Flesh and Bone

Flesh and Bone

An Introduction to Forensic Anthropology

Myriam Nafte

Carolina Academic Press

Durham, North Carolina

ISBN 0-89089-638-0
LCCN 00-108364

Carolina Academic Press
700 Kent Street
Durham, North Carolina 27701
Telephone (919) 489-7486
Fax (919) 493-5668
E-mail: cap@cap-press.com
www.cap-press.com

Printed in the United States of America.

To the Memory of Lisa Shore

Born November 20, 1987
Died October 22, 1998

Contents

Preface

I am the mother of a child who died under mysterious circumstances, and as a result have met and worked with a broad spectrum of forensic investigators—coroners, pathologists, toxicologists, pharmacologists, police, and document examiners. The process of piecing together the events that led to this tragedy could never be undertaken by one person. The efforts and energy of many individuals were integral to the investigative process. It is still ongoing.

Very often a lot is already known about a person who died. Forensic examiners will concentrate on learning about the manner of death, the means of death, who committed the deed, why, and what evidence can be gathered to substantiate their findings.

Sometimes however, the investigation has to begin at a more basic level. Who was the deceased? How old was he or she? Was it a he or a she? What can their bodies tell us about how they died? Forensic anthropologists study human skeletal remains to learn as much information as possible about a deceased person. It is only after they conduct their investigations and studies that others can begin to try and answer other questions.

A perpetrator may attempt to hide evidence by interfering with or relocating human remains, leaving the forensic anthropologist with skeletal parts and fragments. Weather, animal life, insects, soil—the natural environment—all contrive to move, erase, and erode vital evidence. At times, forensic anthropology can be likened to trying to assemble an inordinately complicated puzzle, one with many or most of the pieces missing. It is the forensic anthropologist who must try and put those pieces together in a meaningful way—to reconstruct essential elements of humanity out of anatomic and skeletal remains.

When an individual dies in unusual or suspicious circumstances, whether a child in a hospital (like mine) or an unknown person whose remains are found, we owe to their collective memories an obligation to learn as much as we can about the circumstances of their death. We may find our answers through the efforts of forensic analysis, police investigations, coroner's inquests, and even, occasionally, by the perseverance of the victim's loved ones. These efforts can provide answers to crucial questions, demonstrate ways to avert future tragedies, and help ensure that perpetrators are brought to justice.

Forensic anthropology is an integral part of the meaning—and the method—behind the motto of the Office of the Chief Coroner for Ontario: "We speak for the dead to protect the living."

I cannot adequately express my gratitude to the author for dedicating this book to my late daughter Lisa, and giving me this opportunity to write some words in her memory.

Sharon Shore
www.lisashore.com
August 2000

Acknowledgments

I am indebted to a number of individuals who contributed invaluable time, energy and resources towards the creation of this book. Foremost, my gratitude goes to Dr. Remonda Kleinberg who initiated the idea and got the ball rolling in a significant direction. A very special thanks to John Doucette for allowing me access to the V. Doucette collection, his photographic expertise and inexhaustible efforts to make everything turn out right, and to Angela Milana for dropping everything to photograph collections in various cities. The Office of the Chief Coroner, Toronto Police Services- Forensic Identification Services and the C.A.R.E.S Unit, and the Centre of Forensic Sciences graciously provided case material, resources and pivotal information. Their professionalism and courtesy were inspiring. For giving me access to skeletal collections and/or slide material I must thank the American Academy of Forensic Sciences, Valeri Craigle and The Utah State Office of the Medical Examiner, The Department of Forensic Pathology at the University of Sheffield, Rachel Gropper and Paul Smith of The Michener Institute for Applied Health Sciences, Dr. Max Friesen, Mercedes Doretti of the Argentine Forensic Anthropology Team (EAAF), Dr. Bonnie Chandler, and The Royal Ontario Museum. For the abundant information and resources on teeth, I am grateful to forensic odontologist Dr. George Burgman, and Dr. Ann Dale, curator of The Dental Museum.

As the manuscript unfolded Dr. Shelley Saunders and Dr. Kathryn Denning offered sound research advice and editing suggestions. Howard Kleinberg and Shelagh Lariviere contributed creative editing ideas, while Michelle Hirson did the layout for the forensic science section. Their efforts were critical.

Lastly and most important, I want to thank my husband Keren for the support, guidance and friendship during every stage of this book.

About the Author

Myriam Nafte received an Honours B.A. in Anthropology, and a B.Ed degree from York University. She completed an M.A. in Physical Anthropology at McMaster University in 1992. She has taught college courses in skeletal anatomy, forensic anthropology and archaeology, and she continues to volunteer her services for criminal casework in the United States and Canada.

Introduction

Forensic anthropology is defined here as the analysis of human skeletal remains within the context of a legal investigation.

Using a variety of methods and techniques, forensic anthropologists examine parts of the skeleton, take extensive measurements, and look for particular bumps and grooves on bone. From this process they are usually able to ascertain an individual's sex, approximate age at death, stature and racial origins. They could also determine whether individuals suffered any trauma or disease. Further examination could possibly reveal the health of individuals, whether they were left or right-handed, whether or not they had given birth, and sometimes even their occupation in life.

In the event that skeletal remains are found, providing an analysis of the material may prompt a legal investigation. In one such case a woman came upon some bone fragments and an assortment of teeth while gardening. Thinking that she had uncovered her neighbor's dog burial, she quickly reburied them. However, curiosity got the better of her and she dug them up again to get a closer look. The bones and teeth were brought to a forensic anthropologist and identified as human. Legal authorities were called and an investigation followed. The entire backyard was excavated by police to reveal the scattered remains of a teenaged girl who had gone missing ten years earlier.

Conversely, identifying remains may actually prevent the time and expense of a large-scale legal investigation. In this case a crew of construction workers found bones wrapped in rags and newspaper, along with old shoes and torn shirts stuffed in between the walls of an old house. To the astonished crew, it appeared as if a massacre had taken place. They contacted police who brought the strange assortment to my attention. The assemblage turned out to be a mixture of dog, pig, and horse bones, some crushed and mixed into a form of plaster, and others wrapped in cloth and newspaper, filled with sawdust. According to one of the local farmers, the odd mixture was commonly used as insulation back when the house was first built in the late 1800s.

The discovery of human skeletal remains sets off an immediate series of events once the police are involved. By law, a human body can never be left where it was found. All deaths must be accounted for, and some form of recovery and identification must take place. If the body has decomposed or is skeletonized, recovery and identification are often done by a forensic anthropologist. Any subsequent legal investigation would compel information from a variety of sources, for example from eyewitnesses, suspects, next of kin, and other forensic specialists. Ultimately, the goal is to positively identify the individual and to reconstruct the events surrounding his/her death.

The aim of this book is to give the reader a good background in forensic anthropology by outlining some of the methods and procedures that best define the discipline. It is also designed to introduce readers to the rapidly growing area of forensic science by providing a comprehensive look at many of the participants in the field.

As an introductory guide, the book is an appropriate resource for anthropology and criminology students, individuals in law enforcement, or anyone with an interest in this subject. I avoid technical terminology whenever possible in an effort to keep the reader's attention and interest and to engage those who are working in the field. Technical terms that are used appear in boldfaced type and are explained in the text itself, while references are provided for those with interests in a particular area. The photographs, charts, and illustrations are arranged to complement the text and render it more comprehensible.

All of the chapters begin with their own introduction, and are suited for general understanding. The book follows a logical sequence. Firstly, chapter one discusses all things forensic, which will hopefully clarify many of the misconceptions that exist regarding dead bodies. The broad field of anthropology is defined in chapter two to give one insight as to how a branch of this discipline came to be used as an investigative tool in such a short period of time. Since an examination of human remains is integral to forensic anthropology, chapter three outlines the process of death, decomposition and skeletonization, and chapter four provides a textual and photographic inventory of the human skeleton. The current methods and techniques of examining the human skeleton to determine factors such as sex, age, race, stature, and evidence of trauma are highlighted in chapters five and six. Chapter seven discusses the reconstruction of identity through the process of facial reconstruction, and a detailed description of DNA profiling. Lastly, chapter eight deals with the modern application of forensic anthropology to human rights missions.

There are many graphic photographs depicting human bodies in various stages of decay and which have sustained severe trauma or injury. Out of respect for the victims and their families, the photographs published do not reveal the individual's identity, nor are their case histories discussed. The use of such images in this publication comes with an understanding that the dead need to be honored, not only for the opportunity they have provided for our learning but also in memory of their individual experiences as human beings.

Flesh and Bone

Section I

The Development of a New Discipline

Chapter One

Forensic Science

Chapter One outlines the nature and structure of forensic science, with a short discussion of its legal and scientific associations. Scientists and lawyers did not always get along, and traditionally the courtroom was not the place for scientific discussion. As described in this section, it has taken well over 50 years for the legal system to accept scientific analysis as an essential part of a criminal investigation.

Also in this chapter, the reader is introduced to various legal terms and to the duties of law enforcement officials, investigators, coroners and medical examiners. The text is accompanied with photographs intended to clarify and enhance the discussion.

The field of forensic science is quite comprehensive and its growth over the years complex. For a more detailed look at the history and development of forensics as a science, one can refer to Thorwald, 1965; Thorwald, 1967; Saferstein, 1981; and Gerber, 1983, amongst others.

Science and Public Spaces

Originally, the term *forensic* referred to the place where justice was administered. The word is derived from the Latin word *forum*, *a public space*, as in a market place or meeting ground. *Forensis* thus means *belonging to a public space*, since in Roman times, legal trials, sentencing, and executions were forensic in nature — they were literally for the public to view.

Today we refer to *forensics* as any scientific research aimed at the analysis and interpretation of evidence that is a part of a legal investigative process. Since anything, whether manufactured or occurring in nature, may be considered evidence, forensic science draws from a diversity of disciplines ranging from accounting to zoology. With the integration of methods from such a diverse range of professions, forensic science has developed into a unique field of study. It incorporates research, analysis, interpretation, documentation, and presentation in order to provide the legal system with the factual information it needs.

"Forensic science is the link between the criminal and the crime"

(K.Goddard, 1990)

Science and the Legal System

The use of scientific methods as part of a legal investigation is a relatively new approach to crime solving. During the first half of the last century, science and law were seen as two very separate and distinct fields, frequently at odds with one another. Legal inquiry had little use for the scientist in the courtroom, who was considered more of a meddler than a contributor, although there were many instances where scientists and lawyers worked together successfully on cases (Thomas, 1974; Weihs, 1964; Gerber, 1983, Foster & Huber, 1997).

One reason for the ongoing mutual distrust between science and law was the rapid pace of advances in science, and the legal profession's slow acceptance and understanding of these advances. An example of this dichotomy can be seen in the legal handling of cases regarding paternity, the question of which was always difficult to establish, and impossible to defend. By the mid-1940s, science introduced blood tests for the exclusion of paternity, but courts were cautious to accept the results, and juries were still permitted to choose a mother's testimony over conclusive test results. Vigorous attacks by attorneys and the tears of an unwed mother often won over scientific evidence.

Another reason for the historically inconsistent relationship between science and law was their different practical and conceptual approaches to "fact finding." Lawyers often work under rigid time constraints and adversarial conditions, needing answers as soon as possible without any testing of theories and ideas. Truth is dealt with on a case-by-case basis and ends when the trial concludes. Scientists generally do not work under such predetermined deadlines. They prefer cooperation with their fellow investigators and require elaborate and constant testing of their theories and ideas. The truths sought are more universal, often defying instant explanations and conclusions (Thorwald, 1965; Thomas, 1974).

Though individual scientists and lawyers did work together on specific cases, there was very little cooperation between the professions. Scientists considered it below them to appear in court and present information that could be challenged by non-scientists. Primarily, the police turned to medical schools and physicians for help, especially those with access to a microscope, a novelty item back then with much practical use. Fingerprinting techniques had just developed (1892), along with blood grouping (1898), and a system of performing autopsies, all of which would be applied by a physician with the best equipment. The application of medical expertise to legal investigations was originally referred to as either *forensic medicine, medical jurisprudence,* or *legal medicine.*

The turning point in the relationship between the scientist and the legal system in the United States came in 1948 when Dr. Rutherford Gradwohl of St. Louis organized and chaired a meeting of physicians (the Medico-legal Congress). Scientists from various states and countries such as Canada, Argentina, Cuba, and Chile attended, and the subsequent enthusiasm resulted in the founding of the American Academy of Forensic Sciences (AAFS) that same year. This spawned more organizational meetings with a growing interest in the field of forensics beyond the scope of medicine (Camps et al. 1976).

Fig. 1-1. Photograph of Dr. Gradwohl (Photo, Courtesy of The American Academy of Forensic Sciences).

The AAFS became a professional society by the 1950s, marking the beginning of the modern era of forensic science in the United States. By the 1970s, its membership had broadened to include not only physicians but a wide range of specialists like chemists, psychiatrists, toxicologists, and biologists from around the world.

At the same time, the American Association for the Advancement of Science (AAAS) sponsored a symposium for its annual meeting in 1972. All of the invited speakers were lawyers who had worked with scientists on a variety of legal investigations. The talks focused on how the two professions could work together to fulfill a societal obligation towards justice and crime prevention. The legal system, they pleaded, needed increasing scientific input as crimes were becoming more sophisticated. Speakers demonstrated instances of how scientists had contributed their knowledge and research, which enabled courts to reach decisions and legislators to enact scientifically defensible laws. Scientists attending the symposium were given an overview of the legal process and an appreciation of how essential their contribution was to its function. The objective was to get them, and other technically-trained individuals, to become more actively involved in crime solving.

By the 1990s, the question of whether science was acceptable in the courtroom was no longer applicable. It has since become a question of how forensic science should be conducted on a national level. A series of conferences were initiated by various scientific and legal associations in an attempt to create a standard protocol for scientists who examine evidence and give their expert opinion in a court of law. One particular conference, conducted by the National Institute of Justice in 1999, brought together judges, lawyers, and teams of forensic scientists from across the United States in a landmark effort to establish high standards for forensic experts and to make scientific data more understandable to the justice system.

Presently, the application of scientific expertise to criminal investigation is not only a given, but most often the prerequisite for a successful case. Science and the legal system have consolidated their resources and decided to cooperate and so have created a distinct field that has come to represent the essence of criminal investigation. Law is now increasingly dependent on science and its technology for definitive answers; faster, more exact methods to provide information for use in courts; and the provision of expert testimony (see below). The tolerated meddler had finally become the essential contributor.

Evidence and Expert Witnesses

Almost any field of science and social science may be applied to problems which are presented to legal investigators, criminalists, or lawyers. The process usually begins with the legal investigation of any suspected criminal activity. Police and/or investigators collect evidence from a possible or established crime scene which is then brought to the specialist(s) for analysis, interpretation, and documentation. The nature of the crime and the evidence involved determine the specialist(s) required and the type of documentation and testimony submitted.

The term *evidence* refers to anything that can give or substantiate information in a legal investigation. The word is derived from the Latin word *evidentia*, meaning *to be visible*. The root word from Latin is *videre*, *to see*. Therefore, evidence must often be visible in order to be acceptable and to provide information that may prove or disprove a point in question.

Evidence can be abstract, in the form of information derived from an individual's *testimony* (from the Latin word *testis* meaning *witness*). When individuals *testify*, it is assumed that they do so as witnesses with knowledge or information concerning the case.

Evidence can also be physical, constituting a broader range of items. Indeed physical evidence can be almost anything, from microscopic fibers, paint chips, and insect larvae to vehicles and machinery. Furthermore, due to the development of biological detection systems and more powerful isolation and separation methods, evidence can now be extracted from older, smaller, and more minute substances.

The standard protocol is for police, investigators, or a number of specialists to collect and recover as much evidence as possible from a prospective crime scene. When the evidence has been collected, it is sent by police or investigators to the appropriate facilities for *processing*.

How evidence is processed depends entirely on what needs to be done to it in order to yield factual information. Some physical evidence, as in the case of severely decayed body parts, may need to be defleshed for better analysis, while other forms of physical evidence may require further extraction and closer examination, like bloodstains on clothing or hairs from a sweater. Ultimately, all physical evidence needs to be analysed, test results interpreted, and all gathered information documented. The specialists who process physical evidence for a legal investigation are known as *expert witnesses*, as it is their expertise with that particular form of evidence that provides the information in a court of law. However, because specialists can be drawn from such a diverse group of people, it is ultimately up to a judge, during the trial process, to determine the criteria needed to be declared an expert in a specific field of forensics.

"Physical evidence cannot be wrong, it cannot perjure itself; it cannot be wholly absent; only its interpretation can err. Only human failure to find it, study and understand it can diminish its value"

(Paul Kirk, 1960)

Chain of Custody

Since it is assumed that physical evidence will eventually end up in court, it is necessary to safeguard its transport, handling, labeling, and constant whereabouts. This process of safeguarding physical evidence is referred to as maintaining *the chain of custody*. The concept of a chain of custody—also known as "chain of evidence," "chain of possession," and "continuity of evidence"—is based on the importance of preventing unauthorized persons from accessing, tampering, adding, or altering evidence in any way, from its original discovery right through to its presentation in a court of law. The recipient of evidence must therefore be prepared to keep it secure, account for any access to it, and assume responsibility for its labeling, handling, and transportation. Any indication that there has been an unaccounted-for access to evidence constitutes a "break" in the chain. A break increases the opportunity for evidence to be challenged or rendered inadmissible in court, no matter how damning or scientific it is.

The Forensic Specialists

All disciplines can be called upon to provide information which might be used to solve a legal question or problem in the justice system. As such, there are often many individuals working on one case, collecting and processing evidence. Whatever the discipline involved, if the work involves identifying or processing evidence for a legal investigation, it is called "forensic" work, e.g. *forensic anthropology, forensic odontology, forensic psychiatry, forensic entomology*. Thus the field of forensic science has innumerable possibilities in the way of multidisciplinary contributions.

The goal in involving many specialists during an investigation of suspected criminal activity is the thorough collection and analysis of physical evidence. Many specialists work as a team, relying on each other's expertise to enhance

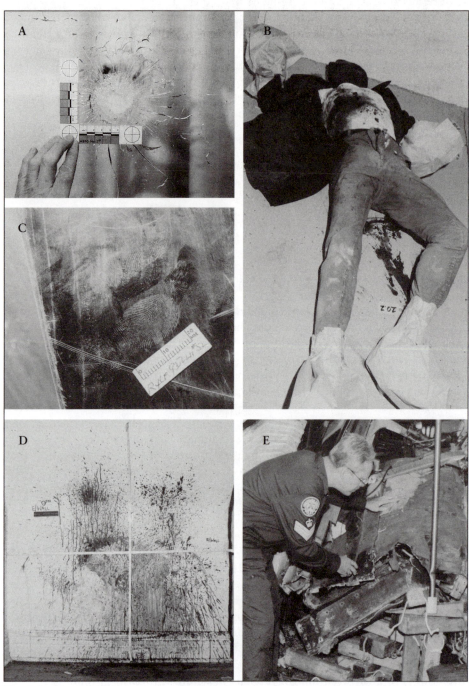

Fig. 1-2. Physical Evidence: A–A bullet hole through glass; B–Death scene, victim's hands and feet are 'bagged' to prevent loss of any trace evidence they may contain; C–The invaluable fingerprint; D–Blood spattering patterns on wall provide crucial evidence; E–A technician examining the remains of a vehicle involved in a collision. Reprinted with permission, Toronto Police Services- Forensic Identification Services, all rights reserved.

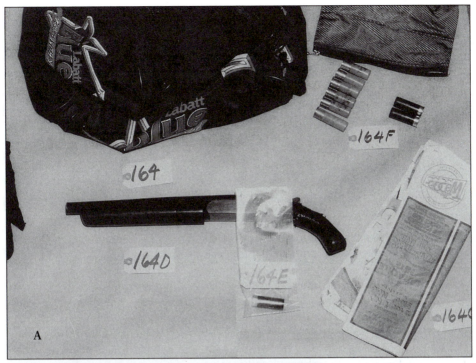

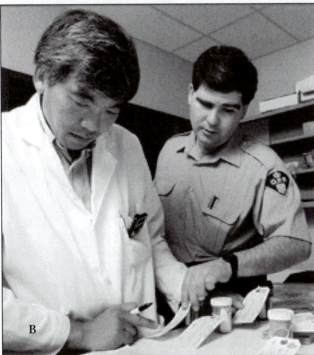

Fig. 1-3. A–Physical evidence that has been seized and tagged for identification. Reprinted with permission, Toronto Police Services-Forensic Identification Services, all rights reserved. B–Forensic scientist signing for the release of evidence delivered by a police officer (Photo, Courtesy of the Centre of Forensic Sciences).

their own understanding of the crime scene and to piece information together. The choice and use of a forensic specialist or team is never a random one, as they are chosen according to the type of evidence which needs analysis. For example, in the case of a shooting death, the firearm's expert is called upon; where bite mark patterns need interpretation, the odontologist is consulted; to determine the approximate time of an individual's death based on the presence of insects, the entomologist is involved; and so on. Their subsequent testimony as expert witnesses, however, must ultimately reflect their own analysis and interpretation of the evidence gathered, not the team's perspective.

The Crime Laboratory

In 1910, Dr. Edmond Locard established a center in France where scientists studying biology, physics, and medicine were brought together to examine evidence for criminal investigations. Together they analyzed a range of material, shared resources and attempted to reconstruct crime scenes. This center came to be known as a *criminalistics laboratory* or *crime lab*. Locard's philosophy (termed *Locard's Exchange Principle*, see below) guided the work within the laboratory and eventually became the foundation for the field of forensic science. The success of Locard's crime laboratory led to the establishment of many others throughout Europe during the early 20th century (Spitz,1993:8).

In North America, the city of Montreal was the first to establish a criminalistics laboratory in 1914, following the Locard model. As it was run by a physician, it came to be known as a *medicolegal* lab and was thus a subspecialty of medicine. Doctors analysed gunshot wounds and fingerprints, and devised a method to establish the presence of alcohol in blood. The structure of the model lab became popular and in the United States the first such laboratory was established in Los Angeles in 1923 by the Los Angeles Sheriff's Department. Soon after that, the newly established Federal Bureau of Investigation set up their own crime laboratory in 1932 which could be accessed nationwide. However, unlike the Locard lab in France, contributions from different areas of science like biology, chemistry and physics, were minimal at this time.

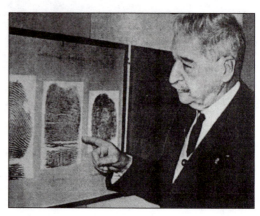

Fig. 1-4. Dr. Edmond Locard (Photo, Courtesy of Institut de Medecine Legale. Lyon, France).

The modern full-service crime laboratory, now also known as a *forensic lab*, typically consists of the following departments: pathology, toxicology, biology, firearms examination, questioned documents, photoanalysis, and chemistry (see pages 14 to 18 for a description of each area). Crime laboratories in the United States that are without these departments or facilities or police stations in more remote parts of the country often send evidential materials to regional crime laboratories or to the FBI's Criminalistics Laboratory in Washington, D.C.

At present, the structure of crime laboratories in the United States varies considerably from state to state. Technically, crime laboratories are under the jurisdiction of the state's law enforcement agency, or a federal agency. But there are privately run laboratories that provide a variety of services as well as crime laboratories operating in universities, public defender's offices, hospitals, and prosecutor's offices.

In an effort to keep track of advances in the field and to establish appropriate standards for crime laboratories across the United States, practicing forensic specialists from around the country have formed various organizations and committees, such as the American Board of Criminalistics, and the American Society of Crime Laboratory Directors. Crime laboratories that wish to be accredited must submit to extensive reviews and examinations by these organizations. The credentials of their personnel, their administrative practices, their use of evidence controls, and the type of examination methods employed are some of the key areas reviewed for accreditation. However, in the United States, this process is voluntary as crime labs do not have to be certified (The National Institute of Standards and Technology Handbook, 1998).

Technology may determine the type and quality of physical evidence available for presentation, but ultimately how evidence is handled and processed by the investigators right through to the forensic laboratory personnel will dictate its admissibility in court.

Locard's Exchange Principle
When any two objects come into contact there is always a transference of material from each object onto another.

(Edmond Locard, ca. 1928)

PATHOLOGY

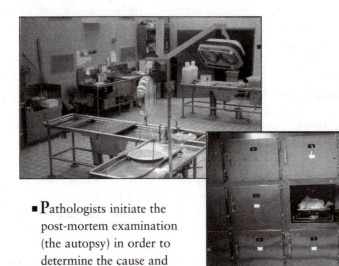

■ Pathologists initiate the post-mortem examination (the autopsy) in order to determine the cause and manner of death.

TOXICOLOGY

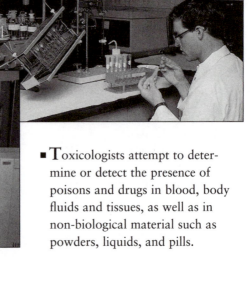

■ Toxicologists attempt to determine or detect the presence of poisons and drugs in blood, body fluids and tissues, as well as in non-biological material such as powders, liquids, and pills.

CHEMISTRY

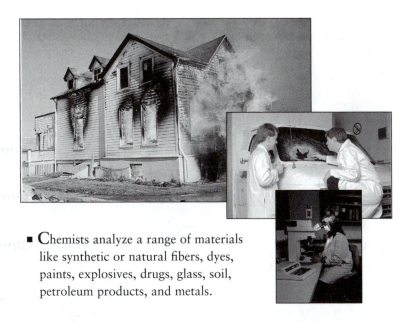

- Chemists analyze a range of materials like synthetic or natural fibers, dyes, paints, explosives, drugs, glass, soil, petroleum products, and metals.

BIOLOGY

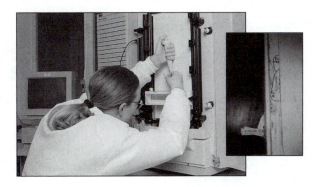

- (Serology and DNA Profiling)
- Serologists seek to identify human and nonhuman biological materials (blood, bodily fluids, hair and fibers) whether they're on items, on individuals or collected from a crime scene.

- DNA Profiling is the analysis of an individual's genetic material derived from bodily fluids, hair, teeth or bone. Profiling is done for comparative analysis and identification purposes.
- Biologists also interpret bloodstain patterns found at crime and accident scenes.

FIREARMS & TOOLMARKS

EXAMINATION

- Firearms experts look at firearms, weapons, remaining live ammunition, fired projectiles and fired cartridge cases, as well as bullets, wound tissue, clothing from shooting victims, tools and tool marks.
- They examine and maintain custody of all evidence resulting from the criminal use of firearms.

DOCUMENTS

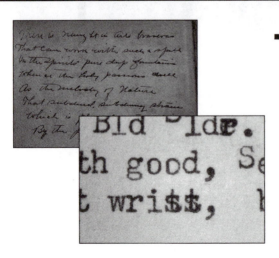

- Document analysts attempt to determine the legality, authenticity or forgery of handwriting, checks, anonymous letters, blackmail notes, ransom and suicide notes. For comparative value, they assess various types of ink and paper, machine-produced documents, and writing instruments.

PHOTOANALYSIS

- **P**hysical evidence is photographed for documentation, presentation, and analysis.
- **A** camera and microscope along with infrared, ultraviolet, x-ray, or laser radiation may be used to highlight details invisible to the naked eye.

ODONTOLOGY (DENTISTRY)

- **O**dontologists examine bite marks, dental impressions, injuries to teeth, dental remains and premortem dental records for comparative and identification purposes.

ENTOMOLOGY

- **E**ntomologists analyze insect activity on human remains as a method of estimating the time and location of death.

ANTHROPOLOGY

- Forensic anthropologists analyze skeletal remains for evidence of trauma and to determine the age, sex, stature, and race of an individual.

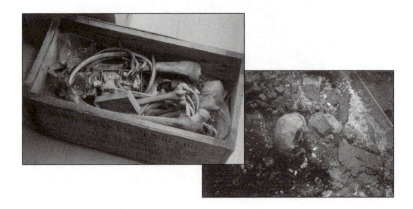

PSYCHIATRY

- Forensic psychiatrists evaluate individuals prior to their trial for the purpose of determining their state of mind, their understanding of the crime committed, and to judge whether they are capable of standing trial.

Bodies, Coroners, and Medical Examiners

The terms *coroner* and *medical examiner* have often been confused by the general public and used synonymously, usually because their activities are rarely defined by the media. Indeed they are both involved with deaths and legal inquiry, but they do have different roles and a different history with the legal investigative process.

The term *coroner* comes from the Latin word *corona*, meaning *crown*. The position was established in England by the 12th century and originally had to do with safeguarding the monetary interests of the King. The coroner was also in charge of handling the relinquished property of felons, murderers, and suicides, hence the early association with crime. Eventually, the responsibility for recording these deaths and keeping track of all criminal matters in the county led to an official position. By the 19th century, the English coroner's function and chief duty was to inquire into the sudden or violent deaths of individuals and to conduct an *inquest* (*a legal inquiry*) to determine the probable cause of such deaths. Early colonists brought this tradition with them to North America.

Currently, the coroner is an elected or appointed official, whose duties still relate to the investigation of the death of any citizen whenever there is suspicion of *foul play* (suspicion that the death occurred as a result of the actions of another, or others). In the United States some state laws do not require that coroners be medical doctors where they are not responsible for directly handling or examining the deceased. Coroner duties are chiefly administrative, primarily focused on consolidating information provided by others involved in a particular case.

Involvement of the coroner usually begins with a deceased human body. Before it can be removed from the site, the police must obtain the permission of the coroner, who decides whether there is to be an inquest. This decision hinges on information provided by the police and other investigators, including interviews with witnesses. The coroner is also empowered by the state to seek out the assistance of any specialist, when necessary, in order to determine the cause of death and to assess whether foul play was in fact involved. If the cause of death is determined to have been as a result of foul play, an inquest is then conducted by the coroner and a jury. The goal of the coroner's inquest is to establish the events and circumstances which led to the death, as well as the immediate cause of the death.

The *medical examiner* is a legally appointed medical doctor, usually one specializing in forensic pathology, who reviews deaths occurring as a result of accident, homicide, and suicide. Any death that is suspicious becomes a case for the medical examiner, who then becomes the central figure in the forensic investigation. The medical examiner visits crime scenes, examines medical and laboratory evidence, and is chiefly responsible for the *autopsy*, the medico-legal examination of the deceased (see below).

In the United States both medico-legal systems—the coroner system and the medical examiner system—are currently in effect. Since there is no federal law requiring that coroners be licensed physicians, certain states give the coroner the right to empower a medical examiner to carry out a medical investigation and conduct autopsies. In other states, the coroner has been entirely replaced by the medical examiner, who is appointed to carry out the same form of investigation. There is no national system requiring medical examiners to be certified as pathologists; hence, in rural communities and remote areas, physicians can act as local medical examiners. In either medico-legal system the point of such administrative duties is to provide judicial authorities with details of cases involving a death. In short, whenever and wherever a death has occurred, the manner and cause must be accounted for by either the coroner, the medical examiner, or both.

The Autopsy

Autopsies are performed for both medical and forensic purposes, and the overall procedures are the same in both areas. However, the focus, goals, and aims of each type of autopsy differ quite substantially.

Medical autopsies are performed by pathologists in hospitals for the purpose of understanding the course and extent of an illness or injury which has led to an individual's death. The individual's identity, the cause of death, and the illness or injury are usually known prior to the autopsy. If they were not known, then the death would have to be referred to the coroner, thereby changing the nature of the autopsy and the people involved. Permission to perform a medical autopsy must be given by individuals with legal control of the body, oftentimes the next-of-kin. The medical autopsy enhances and furthers medical research by providing doctors with an opportunity to observe pathologies and collect biological material (fluids, cells and tissue samples) during the procedure.

Forensic autopsies are performed by pathologists, in conjunction with or by the medical examiner, as part of the legal investigative process. Permission to do so is not required by the next-of kin and can be performed upon the request of the coroner. The primary purpose of the forensic autopsy is to establish the events leading to a death (*manner of death*) as well as the immediate cause (*cause of death*). Special emphasis is placed on establishing the identity of the deceased when possible, determining the approximate place and time of death, and collecting trace evidence. The medical examiner acts in support of criminal investigations by providing this information, usually in the form of a medico-legal report submitted to a district attorney.

The autopsy follows a routine procedure where the body is systematically examined externally and internally. The entire process is thoroughly documented in note form and through dictation, photography and sometimes videotape.

Before external examination begins, radiographs of the body may be taken, blood tests are administered to check the body for any infectious diseases, and fingerprints may be recorded if the fingers are intact. Medical and dental records of missing individuals are evaluated, as they may also help in establishing the identity of the deceased.

During the external examination a description of the deceased is recorded along with any items of clothing, jewelry, or other wrappings. All items removed from the body are documented and carefully transferred for further evidence analysis. Labeling and logging all materials removed from the body are essential in beginning and maintaining the chain of custody. Superficial marks on the body as well as any injuries, tattoos, previous medical treatments, and wounds are assessed and documented. Great care is taken when handling the body, as it may be in an advanced state of decomposition and thereby extremely vulnerable to further damage or loss. Furthermore, body parts, hair, and external cavities may bear trace evidence of considerable importance such as insect larvae, bodily fluids from a different individual, or fibers from a suspect's clothing.

After an external examination is complete, the body is opened up for an internal inspection. If the body is relatively intact, the region that is given the most attention is the head, chest, and abdominal area where the major organs are located. Opening up this area involves sawing open the skull to expose the brain and making a deep Y-incision from the top of both shoulders down the center of the chest to expose the internal organs. A small power saw is used to cut the ribs which are removed for access to the heart and lungs. This method of cutting and removing is known as the **Rokitansky** procedure, after the late 1800s pathologist (Carl von Rokitansky) who developed this form of autopsy.

Visual inspection (macroscopic) involves looking at the overall position of the organs within the body cavities, the walls of the body cavities, and examining the hard and soft tissues (muscle and bones) for evidence of disease, injury, and trauma. Tissue samples are taken from some of these organs for microscopic examination. Organs are then removed from the body, examined, weighed, and measured. Blood or fluid present is measured and documented, and any abnormalities are noted. Tissue samples obtained are also sent to other departments such as toxicology and/or biology for further analysis.

The length, procedure, and goal of the forensic autopsy hinges entirely on the condition of the remains. The process described above is a standard one, performed when the body is relatively intact and not in an advanced state of decomposition. However, if the body is burnt, severely decomposed, in pieces, or skeletonized, then the external examination must be modified and any internal examination is precluded.

Mortui Vivo Docent — the dead teach the living.

(Anonymous)

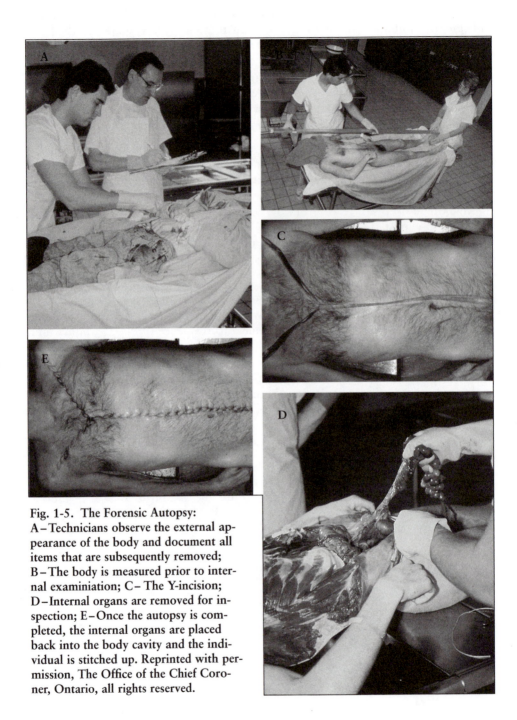

Fig. 1-5. The Forensic Autopsy:
A – Technicians observe the external appearance of the body and document all items that are subsequently removed; B – The body is measured prior to internal examiniation; C – The Y-incision; D – Internal organs are removed for inspection; E – Once the autopsy is completed, the internal organs are placed back into the body cavity and the individual is stitched up. Reprinted with permission, The Office of the Chief Coroner, Ontario, all rights reserved.

Chapter Two

Anthropology

Chapter two provides an introduction to anthropology with a brief description of the subdisciplines that contribute to the field. Some misconceptions surrounding the nature of anthropology and the discipline's unique approach to research and study are explored as a way of understanding the context of forensic anthropology. Following this is a discussion of physical anthropology and the history and development of forensic anthropology beginning with the field's modern era from the 1930s onward. The pivotal research carried out by anthropologists and military personnel in the early part of the last century is described, since most of the tools and techniques used today were developed during this time. Though the anthropologist as expert witness is a recent phenomenon, the scientific contributions of the field have long been recognized. A significant part of anthropology has indeed become a subdiscipline of forensic science, lending a variety of unique approaches and methods to the legal investigative process.

Finally, this chapter concludes with a discussion of the requisite guidelines for investigating the human skeleton as evidence and the role of the forensic anthropologist when involved in legally identifying human remains.

Defining Anthropology

Anthropology, in the public mind, is often associated with archaeology and vague notions of ancient civilizations. As depicted in the media, the archaeologist, the most popularized of the anthropologists, has come to be seen as a heroic figure who uncovers lost cities and treasures while battling fierce natives. Much of what anthropology actually is gets lost in these sorts of erroneous images. Although anthropology does include archaeology, which sometimes does uncover lost cities and treasures, most people are unaware of the breadth of this field.

Generally speaking, anthropology encompasses the entire study of what it means to be human in the past, present, and future. As such, the field is vast and draws from other disciplines, namely the social and natural sciences, at the same time that it explores human nature from a unique perspective— that culture, the natural environment and human biology are seen as constantly interacting forces that physically and socially shape individuals and their societies.

The subfields of anthropology are normally associated with one of two areas, either the *cultural* or the *physical* (see Diagram 2.1) *Archaeology* (the study of material artifacts of past cultures), *linguistics* (the study of language systems) and *ethnology* (the study of present-day societies) are considered cultural approaches to the study of humankind, since patterns of non-biological change are

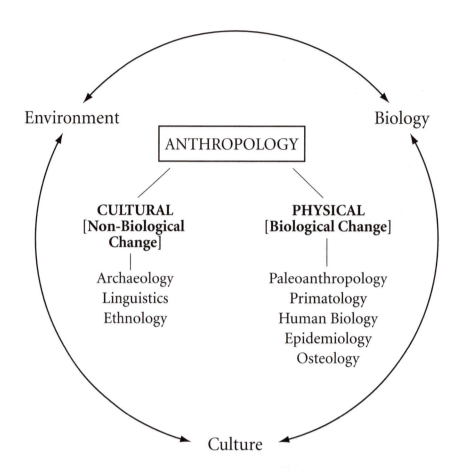

Diagram 2-1. **Anthropology and Its Subfields.** Anthropology explores human nature from a unique perspective- that culture, the natural environment and human biology are seen as constantly interacting forces that physically and socially shape individuals and their societies.

explored. Here *culture* is defined as all the *nongenetic* material that is inherited from one individual, community, or society to the next. Some examples of this type of material are language, customs, behavior, rituals, music, clothing styles, living arrangements, and material goods. Inherited, in this sense, does not intimate that culture is unchanging. In fact, change is a constant and is what anthropologists primarily seek to document.

Paleoanthropology (the study of fossil remains of early primate species), *primatology* (the study of nonhuman primate societies), *human biology* (physical growth, change and adaptability), *epidemiology* (the study of disease), and *osteology* (the study of bones) are the physical approaches to the study of humans. In a nutshell, physical anthropologists examine humans as biological organisms from an evolutionary perspective, that is, within the context of genetic change over time. Though the areas of cultural and physical anthropology are as broad as they are distinct, both emphasize the influence that culture, biology, and the environment have on one another in all human societies past and present.

Physical Anthropology and Forensics

One of the subfields of physical anthropology is *osteology*, an area that explores the physical growth, development, and variation of the human skeleton. Research is based primarily on information gathered from human skeletal populations of the past and present. Skeletal variation, patterns of growth, trauma, genetic vs. cultural influences, anomalies, and pathologies are observed, within and between populations. It is from this area that the tools and methods of forensic anthropology are derived. Hence a *forensic anthropologist* is a physical anthropologist, specifically an *osteologist*, who has become part of the legal investigative process.

Physical anthropologists have assisted with medico-legal investigations over the last 100 years, well before the field of forensic anthropology was officially recognized and its qualifications made standard. During the 1930s and '40s, many physical anthropologists, especially from the Smithsonian Institute, acted as advisors to medico-legal officials through published articles and law enforcement bulletins. These were often in the form of condensed outlines or guides, describing methods of analysis for the purpose of identifying human skeletal remains (See Krogman, 1939; Hooton, 1943; Stewart, 1948 & 1951).

The United States Army called upon physical anthropologists during World War II to identify the skeletal remains of soldiers overseas for repatriation. This led to the establishment of the Central Identification Laboratory (CIL) at the Hickman Air Force Base, Hawaii, in 1947. In 1953, American physical anthropologists participated in the large-scale identification of the Korean War dead. While identifying skeletal remains at the CIL during these two pivotal periods, anthropologists were able to test and develop various methods of analysis (Stewart, 1979:12-15). Research carried out on the war dead also allowed other identification techniques to be advanced and improved (see chapter 5). With the increased participation of physical anthropologists in this form of research and investigation, the field became more formalized.

The term "forensic anthropology" was unheard of prior to the 1970s, although many anthropologists were contributing their services and research to forensic matters. Wilton M. Krogman is often cited as the founder of modern forensic anthropology since most of his research and writing were directed towards assisting medicolegal personnel. His initial *Guide to the identification of human skeletal material,* published in 1939 as an FBI Bulletin, was the first of its kind and provided an important source for identifying human skeletal remains in both legal and military contexts. Thomas D. Stewart, a physical anthropologist at the Smithsonian Institute during the 1940s and 50s, acted as a consultant for the FBI and then applied his research methods in assessing the Korean War dead. Krogman and Stewart, from the 1940s through to the 1970s, devoted a considerable amount of research and writing to the forensic applications of physical anthropological methods (Krogman, 1943; Krogman, 1962; McKern & Stewart, 1957; Stewart,1970; Stewart, 1979). In the 1960s, Lawrence Angel joined the Smithsonian staff and continued the role of consultant for the FBI, launching a training program for the forensic applications of skeletal biology. Such efforts, along with the increase in applying osteological research methods for forensic cases, culminated in the founding of a physical anthropology section in the American Academy of Forensic Sciences (AAFS) in 1972 (Stewart, 1979; İşcan, 1981a).

Since the establishment of a physical anthropology section in the American Academy of Forensic Sciences, there has been a dramatic shift in terminology. Since membership as a physical anthropologist in the AAFS exclusively entailed forensic applications, they were no longer referred to as physical anthropologists. Hence, all 14 members in 1972 became known as *forensic anthropologists*. Subsequently, the American Board of Forensic Anthropology (ABFA) was established in 1977, sponsored by the AAFS and the Forensic Sciences Foundation. The founding of the Academy as well as the Board was a direct response for the increased need to identify and certify qualified physical anthropologists throughout North America specifically for forensic work. The discipline grew rapidly in the 1970s and 80s as participants became highly specialized, issuing a range of laboratory manuals, guides, handbooks, and papers on specific methods and techniques. Following Krogman and Stewart's lead, publications outlining the role of the forensic anthropologist became numerous. High profile cases, mass disasters, and media attention over the last two decades have also served to increase the discipline's status and the general public's awareness of the field; not to mention its popularization in crime fiction writing (See Reichs, 1999) and personal memoirs (See Maples, 1995; Rhine, 1998). As such, the forensic anthropologist's earlier role as a consultant on sporadic cases evolved to that of an essential authority on all things relating to skeletal identification.

Most forensic anthropologists in North America are physical anthropologists with graduate training in human osteology. The forensic applications of human osteology are not usually part of a graduate degree since osteological training within the scope of physical anthropology inherently offers the scientific techniques applicable to identifying human remains within a legal investigation. Programs and training in some universities, however, have increasingly offered specialties in radiography, law, DNA analysis, and crime scene investigation, which have served to broaden the field's interests and requirements.

As forensic anthropology becomes more specialized, and increasingly incorporates techniques from other areas of forensic science and criminology combined with the requirements of the ABFA, physical and forensic anthropology seem likely to become separate subfields altogether. With the establishment of the American Board of Forensic Anthropology, a regulatory and certification system allows physical anthropologists with an interest in applying their skills for judicial purposes to have official recognition, support, and promotion. As a result, forensic anthropology has become the only subfield within anthropology to have a process of board certification. Furthermore, handling and processing physical evidence and understanding the role of the expert witness when giving testimony are not parts of the physical anthropologist's training as they are a forensic anthropologist's. Though the shared methods, tools and techniques continue to define physical and forensic anthropology as one and the same, their varying interests, field experiences, and levels of participation have created distinct approaches, applications, and research goals for each.

Fig. 2-1. Physical anthropology students assessing human skeletal material (Photo, Angela Milana).

Defining Forensic Anthropology

Forensic anthropology involves the processing and analyzing of human skeletal remains within the context of a legal investigation. Human bodies that are found in stages of advanced decomposition or as complete skeletons often preclude an autopsy, which is primarily an analysis of the soft tissues and organs. Hence, decomposed or skeletal remains are typically turned over by the police or coroner to forensic anthropologists for analysis. They, in turn, participate in the investigative process by assessing the remains in order to determine the individual's age, race, sex, and stature (chapter five offers a detailed discussion of the methods and techniques involved).

When a crime has been committed, skeletal remains are considered physical evidence. The forensic anthropologist must therefore be prepared to give information as an expert witness, in the form of testimony (verbal or documented) on the state of the remains. They primarily assign the remains a *biological* identity (age, sex, race, and stature), comment on whether there was damage to the skeleton, the likely objects that produced the damage, and whether it was sustained prior to or after death. The manner and cause of death are usually not a part of the forensic anthropologist's analysis or testimony, since these questions cannot be answered with scientific certainty. For example, death could have come about without having left a mark on the individual's skeleton, and conversely, an individual could survive massive bone trauma without it ultimately having caused his/her death.

The work of forensic anthropologists is not always limited to an analysis in a lab. Along with the challenges of processing and analyzing skeletal remains, they are often asked to assist in locating and recovering the remains, as well as inter-

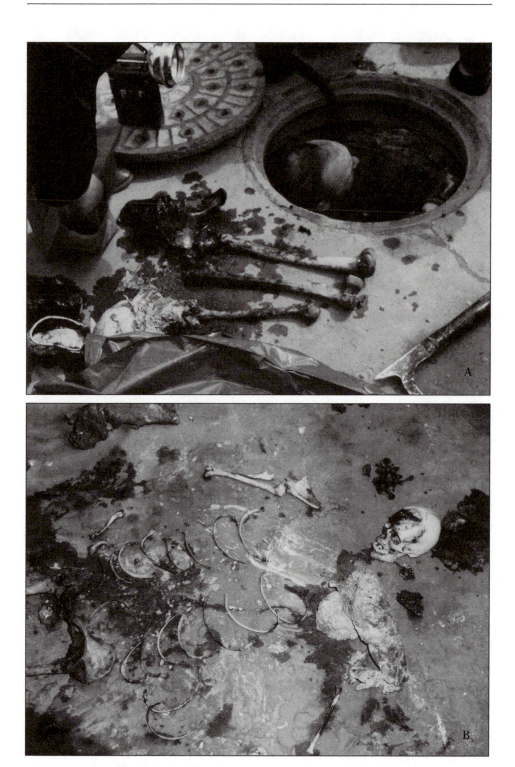

Fig. 2-2. A – Human remains are recovered from a sewer; B – Skeletal remains are assembled on site after recovery (Photos, Courtesy of The V. Doucette Collection).

preting any *ante, peri* and *postmortem* (before, during, and after death) movements or modifications. An analysis of the scene or site, in which the remains have been found may also be required. Such an extensive involvement entails that the forensic anthropologist must also be responsible for recognizing, recovering, and preserving materials (as in bodily fluids, soft tissue, clothing, soil, and insects) for other analysts.

Though forensic anthropologists predominantly study skeletonized cases, they may also examine fresh, decomposed, burned, or mummified remains, as well as premortem dental and medical records. As a result, they participate in a wide variety of scene investigations and cases, such as serial murders, multiple-fatality incidents, mass disasters, cremations, and animal scavenging.

Wherever and whatever human remains are uncovered, the methods employed in their recovery and assessment determine the reliability and success with which the case is resolved. The remains themselves may constitute the only physical evidence available that may contribute to the apprehension and conviction of the person or persons responsible for their deposition. Therefore their proper handling, transportation, documentation, and assessment are all critical components in the work of the forensic anthropologist.

The Human Skeleton as Evidence

Skeletal remains are discovered in many ways, and in various condition. People walking their dogs, gardening, hiking, or hunting have often come upon them in rural areas, backyards, and city centers. Since all known or suspected human bones are protected by laws throughout the U.S. and Canada, it is a punishable offense to pick them up or remove them from their site. The discoverer is required by law to contact the authorities. The police are usually the first ones called to the scene as they are legally empowered by the coroner or medical examiner to secure the site, call in an appropriate recovery unit, take possession of the remains, and attempt to have them identified.

When forensic anthropologists are asked to assist, they first try to answer the following three questions in order to determine whether the bones are of forensic significance.

1) Are the Remains Bone?

Damaged bone, after having been chewed or burned, crushed or cut, can be difficult to identify or even recognize. Conversely, certain materials like burned asbestos, bits of melted foam insulation, certain types of petroleum products, tree-root segments, and shell can all be mistaken for bone fragments. When superficial examination is not adequate, observing the questionable material under a microscope will help. If it is found to be bone, the next question is posed.

2) Are the Remains Human?

Human skeletal remains are often confused with animal remains and vice versa. When a human adult skeleton is fully articulated (intact) and has not been scattered or disturbed, it is easily recognizable, especially if there is a skull remaining. However, this situation is rare. Forensic investigations generally encounter scattered remains on the surface of the ground more frequently than intact, buried remains (Haglund, 1998:42). This means that the opportunity for error is greater.

The difficulties in identification arise when remains have been scattered and damaged. Long bones missing joint surfaces, the small bones of the hands and feet, and vertebrae are seldom recognizable when they have been burned or damaged. Microscopic analysis can reveal whether the bits of bone were indeed human.

Bones discovered in rural settings are most often animal bones. When their distinctive joint surfaces are intact they are easily identified. However, there are occasions where certain animal bones look very similar to human bones, especially when there are remnants of flesh or muscle attached. The fore and hind paws of bears that have been skinned look very similar to human hand and foot bones; the lower vertebrae of a horse's tail look similar to human finger bones; and deer vertebrae are similar in size and shape to human vertebrae

In the case where there are human fetal or infant bones, identification can be confusing to the non-specialist. Fetal and juvenile bones are undeveloped and small, with a different *morphology* (shape) from adult bone and can easily be mistaken for nonhuman animal remains (see chapter 5).

If the bones are found to be human, the next question must be posed before a legal investigation proceeds.

3) Are the Human Remains Ancient, Historic, or Modern?

If the remains have been identified as human, it is critical to determine their age. Were they deposited there recently, a hundred years ago, or three thousand years ago? Many clues may indicate whether remains are *ancient* (in a North American context, over approximately 500 years old), *historic* (approximately 100 to 500 years) or *modern* (within the last 50 years).

The investigation of the area surrounding the remains is the first step in establishing the temporal context of skeletal material. The location of the site is the first logical consideration. One must research or observe whether there are archaeological sites nearby, prehistoric or historic burial grounds, and if the area is a largely secluded and undisturbed one. In a large and developed urban center, surface remains that have been discovered behind factories, in parking lots, off highways, and in apartment buildings are not often ancient or historic unless they have been deposited there by a modern population. There are always exceptions to this, however. If the remains are found buried in undisturbed soil, rural

Fig. 2-3. A–Sorting through animal remains (Photo, Angela Milana); B–A mixture of both human and animal remains apparent to the trained eye (Photo, John Doucette).

areas, or remote regions, there is an increased chance that they are historic or ancient.

The context of the surface find or burial is important. Are there clothing and items associated with the remains? Are there clay, shell, or glass beads? Are hunting implements like stone or bone arrowheads, decayed animal skin, or clay potsherds buried or scattered within the vicinity? The presence of any of these items could indicate ancient Native American remains, rendering the site archaeologically significant. Alternatively, is there personal identification, a watch, money, or bits of clothing available that could date the site? If the remains were found on the surface of the ground and they still contain freshly decomposed flesh, hair, and clothing, or if there is insect activity, then the remains are often very recent.

Nonetheless, the context of the site may not always correspond with the skeletal remains. An individual could have been deposited on an ancient site, or disturbed ancient remains could have been left somewhere in the midst of a city. Since there are many variations to imagine, the investigation of the site surrounding the remains (the search area) must be thorough.

The condition, color, and shape of the skeletal material can indicate whether the remains are ancient, historic, or modern. Ancient bones that have been buried, for example, may be more stained and decayed due to soil leeching. The wear patterns of the teeth, the morphology of the dental incisors, and the shape of the long bones can be reliable indicators of ancient Native skeletal remains (Brothwell, 1983; Ubelaker, 1989). Historic remains may contain implements, injuries, and/or evidence of surgical procedures that reflect the time period, such as old prosthetic limbs, tin fillings, ivory dentures, and gold wire. However, the presence of dental work such as amalgam tooth fillings, caps, crowns, and bridges, as well as orthopedic implements like long bone pins, metal plates, screws, and hip replacement heads, are obvious indicators that the remains are relatively modern.

Determining the temporal nature of the skeletal remains is pivotal as this will dictate the direction of the investigation. If the remains are found to be ancient, or historic, they are not of forensic significance and are therefore not investigated further within the next set of procedures. Native remains, from either of these periods, are legally protected under the Native American Graves Protection and Repatriation Act (NAGPRA) of 1990. Before Native remains can be removed or reburied, any investigator, coroner, or medical examiner must notify the nearest Native American/Canadian group in order to offer them the opportunity to claim the remains. Nonnative historic remains are often turned over to academic or museum facilities for assessment and safekeeping, unless they are associated with a specific cemetery, in which case they are simply reburied.

If the remains are found to be modern, they are of forensic significance. This is based on the premise that the deaths of all individuals which occur in the United States and Canada within a particular time period must be accounted for. Hence, their remains— intact, decomposed or skeletonized—are protected under the law, prior to and during any subsequent investigation. A legal investigation into the identity of the individual, the possible time, place, and cause of their death, and the events leading up to the deposition of their remains can then proceed.

Skeletal Recovery

Recovering human skeletal remains from a possible crime scene and preparing them for transport often represent the first steps of a forensic anthropologist's involvement. Found bones are never randomly collected or pulled up from the position in which they were discovered. A thorough recovery operation involves

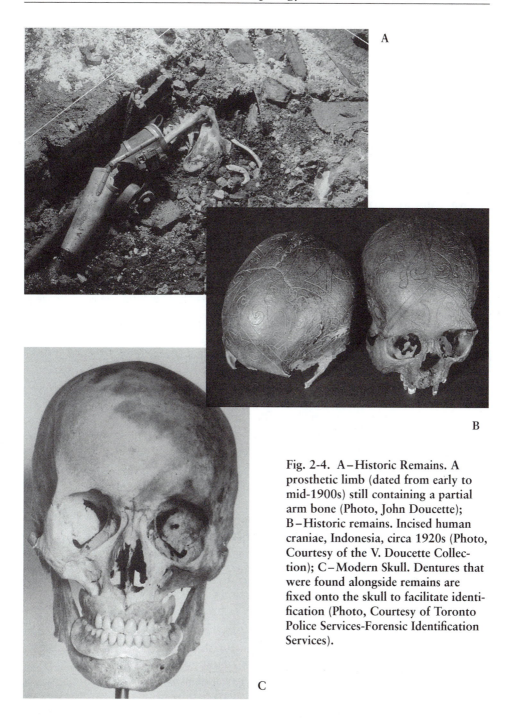

Fig. 2-4. A–Historic Remains. A prosthetic limb (dated from early to mid-1900s) still containing a partial arm bone (Photo, John Doucette); B–Historic remains. Incised human craniae, Indonesia, circa 1920s (Photo, Courtesy of the V. Doucette Collection); C–Modern Skull. Dentures that were found alongside remains are fixed onto the skull to facilitate identification (Photo, Courtesy of Toronto Police Services-Forensic Identification Services).

mapping, photographing and/or videotaping, searching the sites in and around the remains, and collecting, packing, and transporting all of the associated evidence.

The forensic anthropologist with training in archaeology has a distinct advantage in recovery procedures, as many of the tools and methods used in locating human remains are those used for archaeological excavations, such as ground surveying, penetrating radar, aerial photography, and the proton magnetometer. Also, the process of excavating and packing human remains usually follows an archaeological standard (Haglund, 1998; Brothwell, 1981; Bass & Birkby, 1978).

The nature of the investigation and a variety of constraints such as weather, budget, geography, equipment, resources, and legal issues often dictate a forensic anthropologist's level of involvement. Hence, he/she may not always have the opportunity to recover or see the remains *in situ* (where they were originally found).

Most anthropologists prefer to be part of the recovery and excavation whenever possible, as this gives them the opportunity to analyze and interpret the remains in their original state, document their finds, and keep track of the skeletal material leaving the site. It also gives them the opportunity to ensure that nothing is lost or left behind as it can be easy to miss material like cremated bits of bone, teeth, and immature remains. Other anthropologists feel that assessing the remains in a lab away from the original site, allows them to analyze the *decedent* (the dead individual) more objectively and solely on the basis of "what the bones tell them"(Stewart, 1979:31-32).

In a large urban center with higher crime rates, or in remote areas with difficult access, it may not always be feasible to immediately obtain the services of a forensic anthropologist. Likewise, remains that have been found, disturbed, and brought in by curious individuals preclude an onsite recovery. In any case, how and where the remains come to be in the possession of the forensic anthropologist will be secondary to their subsequent assessment, as long as their handling, whereabouts, and transport have been consistent and the chain of custody not broken.

Skeletal Inventory

Prior to any physical analysis, forensic anthropologists must first sort through the remains that have been recovered and/or delivered. They make an inventory, most often in a simple checklist fashion, to establish what bones are present.

Bones that are missing pose many questions that can be difficult to answer if the forensic anthropologist did not see the original site or recover the material. Scattered and missing skeletal material can be due to animal scavenging; gravity; weather conditions such as winds, snow melt, and water flow; the deliberate action of a perpetrator; the oversight of an excavator; or some or all of the above. The advantage of being part of the initial recovery process is that any missing skeletal material can be tracked from the outset, rather than questioned as lost or left behind. An incomplete recovery ultimately compromises an investigation.

Inventories are also important in establishing whether there is more than one individual present, that is whether there is *commingling* of human or nonhuman skeletal material. The question of commingling depends however on the type of bones present. It is not abnormal for an individual to have, for example, an extra vertebra or rib, and an assortment of small bones that grow within tendons (*sesamoid* bones). In contrast, the presence of two left femurs (bones of the thigh), or of other limbs or skulls, are normally indicative of commingling. One must also assess whether the extra bones are human or animal as it is not unusual for there to be both, especially in animal lairs and dens.

After the remains have been sorted and categorized, the next step is to establish a biological profile of the individual(s). In the event of a judicial process, the biological profile will be the information presented by the forensic anthropologist as testimony in a court of law.

The Forensic Anthropologist as Expert Witness

When forensic anthropologists examine and identity human remains for a legal investigation, they immediately commit themselves to the possibility of appearing as an expert witness in a court of law. The obligation to do so is reflected in the *subpoena* which is issued to them and any other persons involved with the processing of evidence. A subpoena (Latin for *under pain* or *penalty*) refers to the command from a court of justice to appear before the court to present testimony. Failure to appear can result in some form of penalty.

The role of the forensic anthropologist as an expert witness is to be impartial and to present the results of their assessment. Statements regarding the age range, stature, sex, and race of the human remains constitute the bulk of testimony. There may also be cause to cite the condition of the remains, and the presence of any marks, fractures, breaks, burns, cuts, or chew marks. Since absolute certainty is rarely reached, especially when skeletal parts are missing or damaged, the information is presented as probable, with the likelihood of error.

Determining the *biological* identity (age, stature, sex, race) of the skeletal remains is the primary responsibility of the forensic anthropologist. The testimony itself does not set out to prove that the remains are those of a certain individual or to cite the manner or cause of death. Establishing an individual's *social* identity (their name, place and date of birth) and the means by which they met their fate is up to the investigative team, and ultimately a jury.

When skeletal remains and the associated evidence suggest a homicide, the testimony of the forensic anthropologist is important in helping to establish what is called the *corpus delicti,* (Latin for *the body of crime)*. In this case, the *corpus delicti* refers to the individual's physical body. The testimony designates the facts surrounding the death of the person alleged to have been murdered. It may be composed of information such as premortem medical and/or dental records, facial reconstruction, or DNA results that would illustrate the probability of the skeletal remains being those of the murdered individual. The cause and manner of death would not be ascertained by the forensic anthropologist; rather, the condition of the remains would be used to illustrate the possibility of certain events having taken place, for example, gunshot penetrations and fractures, cutting marks, knife penetrations, and cremation. In other words, any part of the skeletal remains that appears to conform to the description of the alleged murder victim and the events which led to his/her death, may be assessed as the *corpus delicti*.

Human skeletal remains may constitute physical evidence when an individual's death is of a suspicious nature, but most importantly they are human remains. Therefore, unlike other forms of physical evidence, they will not be part of an exhibit for the courtroom. Family or community members may even have the remains interred by the time the case comes to trial. The forensic anthropologist must provide a well-documented analysis or conclusion by way of verbal testimony, written statements, and/or photographs and slides of the skeletal features they wish to highlight. Since the jury cannot directly handle or observe human remains *in situ* or in the courtroom, it is up to the forensic anthropologist to bring to life, so to speak, the individual's human identity and the condition of the skeletal remains.

Section II

The Human Body

Chapter Three

Flesh and Bone— The Process of Decomposition

Forensic anthropologists are increasingly being asked to determine the *post-mortem interval* (the time of death) when investigating cases. However, skeletal remains and those still with flesh are difficult to assess with scientific certainty. Estimates of the time of death are therefore applied within a range of days, months, or years as opposed to minutes and hours (Sledzik, 1998). But the range becomes more inaccurate as the time interval since death increases.

The human body, like all animals with flesh, decomposes. Biologically, it breaks down and decays, until it is eventually a skeleton. This process occurs in stages, all of which are affected by physical and environmental variables (see Tables 3-4 and 3-5).

Understanding the stages of decomposition under various conditions is helpful for descriptive and comparative purposes, but the stages themselves do not render an absolute time of death (Micozzi, 1991). Decomposition is a sequential and somewhat predictable process, however the duration of the process is not. For example, a body can be reduced to bones within days in hot, humid areas with high insect activity, but the same process may take hundreds of years in the case of frozen bodies. As such, the postmortem interval is often an educated guess offered by the forensic anthropologist when physical and environmental variables are considered along with prior experience, research from controlled studies, and the assistance of other specialists from the death scene (Galloway, 1998; Rodriguez & Bass, 1983; Mann et al., 1990).

The following is an overview of the stages of late postmortem change, the process of decomposition, and the physical and environmental variables which affect both. The discussion will be limited to bodies which have not been embalmed, as embalming is a procedure that delays or in many cases, prevents decomposition (Sledzik and Micozzi,1997).

Defining Death

From a biological perspective, death is not a definitive event but a continuous process that occurs over a period of time.

When cardiac activity stops and respiration, reflexes, movement, and brain activity cease, this is referred to as *somatic death*. Muscles, organs, tissues, and cells then begin to break down and die at different intervals, which can vary from 3 minutes to a few hours. Complex chemical reactions take place and certain enzymes are activated. The blood becomes acidic and begins to clot.

When metabolism eventually ceases and all the cells in the body are dead, *autolysis* (cellular death) has occurred. The time frame within which autolysis occurs is largely dependent on environmental factors. The higher the temperature, the faster cellular death occurs as the chemical changes taking place are accelerated by heat. During and after the stages of cellular death, the biochemical process of decomposition begins and, if uninterrupted, will continue until the body is completely skeletonized.

Table 3-1: The Process of Death

Somatic Death	*Cellular Death (Autolysis)*
– cardiac activity stops	– metabolism ceases
– respiration, reflexes, and movement cease	– all cells in the body are dead
– no brain activity	

Estimating Time of Death — The "Mortises"

When somatic death occurs and the process of cellular death begins, late postmortem changes set in. The enzymatic changes and biochemical reactions taking place in the human body give rise to three conditions known as algor, livor, and rigor mortis. These conditions usually occur simultaneously, beginning in the first two to four hours after death and continuing until approximately 48 hours (see Table 3-2).

Algor mortis (*algor*–Latin for "cold," *mortis* "deadly") is the stage where the body begins to lose heat and its core temperature of 98.6°F (37°C) falls to that of the surrounding environment. If death occurs in a hot environment however, the core body temperature will rise. The amount of heat loss or gain is highly variable and depends on factors such as the temperature of the body before death, the temperature of the surrounding environment, the type of clothing on the individual, and the size of the body.

The time of death, based on the development of algor mortis, can be estimated by measuring the core body temperature, since it falls at a theoretically predictable rate (approximately 1.5°F per hour), and comparing it to the ambient temperature. However, the variables listed above must be considered as they limit time of death estimates to approximations. In other words, the time it takes for a core body temperature to reach that of its surrounding environment will vary from almost no time to just over two hours, depending on the individual and the environment.

While the core temperature of a body is falling, blood high in acidity begins to clot in areas that are free of any pressure. This clotting produces a dark, bruise-like coloring. The parts of the body that are restricted by pressure from items such as tight clothing or hard surfaces, are often lighter or blanched as blood cannot settle in these areas. The patterns of bruising and blanching on the body as a result of blood clotting is a condition referred to as *livor mortis* (*livor*–Latin for *bluish color*).

The Process of Decomposition 41

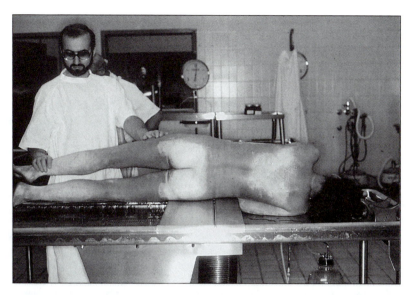

Fig. 3-1. Livor Mortis. Reprinted with permission, The Office of The Chief Coroner, Ontario, all rights reserved.

Blood begins to settle as soon as 15 to 20 minutes after death and livor mortis can be detected then by the trained professional. However, it is usually not evident until at least two hours after somatic death. Livor mortis advances further with clotted areas darkening, and eventually becomes fixed approximately four to six hours after death.

The onset of livor mortis is used to assess the postmortem interval but is also useful for determining the position of the body at the time of death. For example, if the patterning of the blanch marks do not correspond with the position that the body was found in, it can be assumed that the body had been moved from its original site some time after death occurred.

While blood is clotting and settling, muscle cells cease aerobic functioning. Oxygen is no longer available so muscle cells function anaerobically. As a result there is a build up of lactic acid in the muscle tissue, which in turn causes a chemical reaction. The proteins (actin and myosin) in the muscle begin to fuse and form a gel-like substance. The presence of this gel in muscle tissue creates a stiffness throughout the body. This state is referred to as ***rigor mortis*** (*rigor*–Latin for *stiff*).

Rigor mortis initially invades small muscle groups, like the face and hands, within two to four hours after death. Gradually it works its way into larger muscles within a 24 hour period, after which the entire body will be in a state of rigor and remain so for at least 24 to 48 hours. After the 48 hour period, chemicals in the muscle cells are consumed, coagulated blood thins out (re-liquefies) and rigor mortis dissipates leaving the body flaccid once again.

The time in which it takes for rigor mortis to set in is determined by several factors. In a hot environment, in the very young, in the very old, or when an individual has an increased body temperature due to a fever, the onset of the rigor will be much faster and will last for a shorter period of time. Physical activity like running or vigorous exercise just prior to death increases lactic acid levels

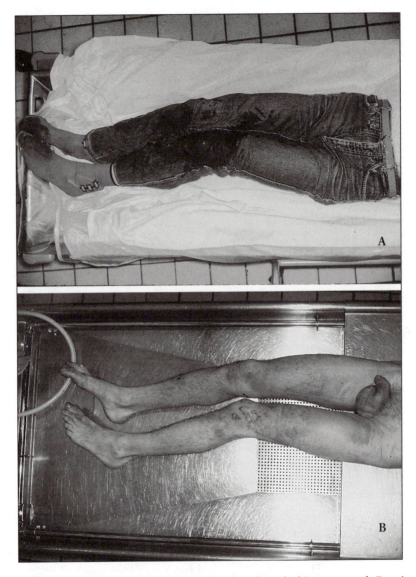

Fig. 3-2 A-B. Rigor mortis apparent in lower limbs when clothing removed. Reprinted with permission, The Office of The Chief Coroner, Ontario, all rights reserved.

which also leads to a faster onset of rigor. Conversely, heavier and more seden-tary individuals with normal body temperatures have a slower rate of onset and a longer period of duration.

Though algor, livor, and rigor mortis occur simultaneously, they are indepen-dent of one another. Physical and environmental factors will interfere with their onset and duration, delaying or prolonging them in an unpredictable way. There-fore, estimates of the postmortem interval within the 48 hour period in which they occur are not exact, but fairly reliable because of the relatively short period of time that has elapsed since death. Estimates based on these late postmortem changes beyond the 48 hour time frame, will vary in accuracy and become less reliable as decomposition advances.

Table 3-2: Late Postmortem Changes

Postmortem State	Time Elapsed Since Death	Characteristics
Algor mortis	0-2 hours	– body loses heat
		– core body temperature falls to that of the surrounding environment
Livor mortis	1-4 hours	– blood clotting
		– bruising/blanching become evident
		– blood coagulates
		– livor mortis becomes fixed approx. 4-6 hours after death
Rigor mortis	2-4 hours	– lactic acid build up in muscle tissue
		– proteins in muscle begin to fuse
		– muscle groups stiffen
		– stiffening dissipates after 24-48 hours

Decomposition

Decomposition can be organized into stages according to the nature of the internal and external changes taking place. The sequence of these changes is somewhat consistent if the body is left undisturbed. However, the rate at which these changes take place is directly related to the condition of the body at death and the quality and time of the body's exposure to factors such as climate, soil composition, and insect activity (see Tables 3-4 and 3-5). For example, in hot, humid climates the stages of decomposition can take a matter of days, whereas in cold, dry climates it can take many years. Understanding the stages of decomposition for the purpose of estimating the postmortem interval is based on a consideration of these factors, their interplay, and how they vary throughout North America.

Initial decomposition begins internally caused by microorganisms already present in the body. While the body's external appearance may still seem fresh, organisms like bacteria and protozoa become active and multiply rapidly throughout the intestinal tract. Gases are produced as byproducts of this activity, causing the intestinal tract to swell and rupture. The entire body becomes bloated with the pressure of this internal gas and eventually collapses, leaking what is referred to as *purge fluid*. During this stage the body gives off very strong and distinct odors, caused by intensive microbial activity, indicating that it is in a state of putrefaction. The exposed flesh blackens and the internal organs and tissues take on a creamy consistency. This stage is known as *black putrefaction*. The body then hastens towards fermentation and moulding, referred to as *butyric fermentation*. The remaining flesh at this point is of a cheesy consistency and is slowly hardening and drying. Eventually it *desiccates* (dries up) during the stage of *dry decay*.

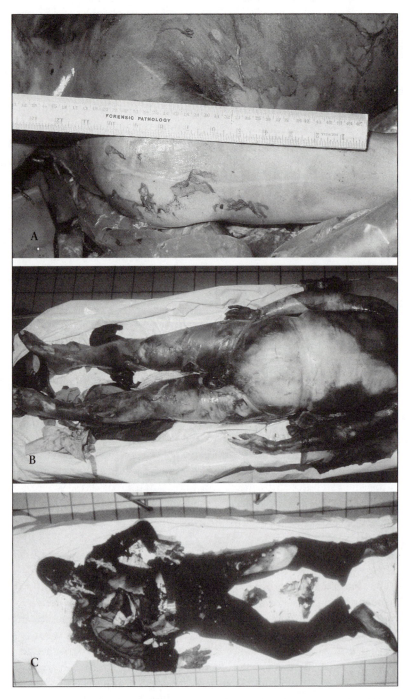

Fig. 3-3. Decomposition. Reprinted with permission, The Office of The Chief Coroner, Ontario, all rights reserved. A–Initial Decay; B–Bloating apparent in abdominal region; C–Decomposition is moderate to advanced.

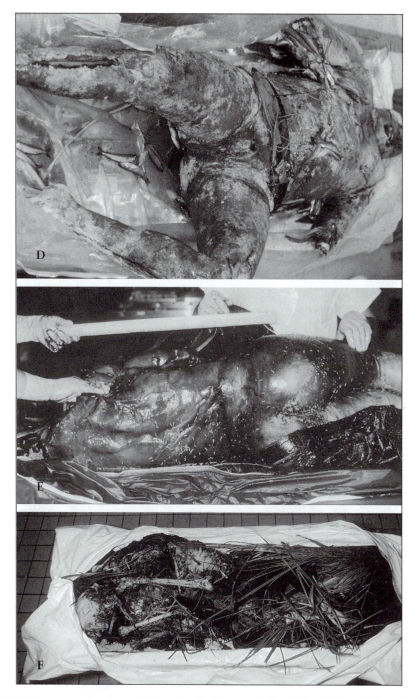

Fig. 3-3. Decomposition (cont.). Reprinted with permission, The Office of The Chief Coroner, Ontario, all rights reserved. D – Body in state of putrefaction (pulled from water); E – Black putrefaction (insect activity is rampant); F – Decomposition is advanced, skeletonization is apparent.

A soft, whitish substance may become evident on the body during the decaying process. If the body had been submerged in water, or contains water and a lot of fatty tissue, a layer of what is referred to as *adipocere* (*adipo*-Latin for "fat" and *cere* "wax") forms over some soft tissue and bone. This is caused by the formation of fatty acids through the hydrolysis and hydrogenation of body fats (a chemical reaction involving water that essentially converts body fat to fatty acids). Though adipocere formation can occur only a few days after death, it does not become visible for at least 3 months. Once formed however, it is relatively permanent and may preserve surface features of the body for years if left undisturbed.

Skeletonization

The final stage of decomposition is known as skeletonization. This occurs when most, if not all, of the soft tissue is gone, exposing the bone. Ligaments, tendons, and cartilage are usually still intact after flesh and muscle decay. These may dry, crack, and then eventually disintegrate, depending on environmental factors. Bones at this stage may have a greasy texture indicating that there is still fatty tissue present. Greasy bones with a brown to dark yellow color represent remains that are months old. Fatty tissue dries up and bones *blanch* (whiten) if exposed to sunlight. Bones which have been exposed to the elements for years may crack and chip (exfoliate). If bones are buried they may absorb the soil contents and become stained. In acidic soils they may disintegrate altogether.

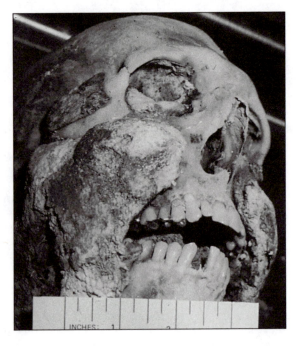

Fig. 3-4. Human skull showing adipocere. Reprinted with permission, The Utah State Office of the Medical Examiner, all rights reserved.

Like the postmortem changes and the initial stages of decomposition, many factors determine the rate at which skeletonization and bone decomposition take place. For instance, if a body is buried in acidic soil in a warm, humid climate, skeletonization can take place within a two week period (Stewart,1979;71). In a body that has been left exposed on the ground in a cold, dry environment, the process can take years. In an arid outdoor climate, it can take anywhere from 5 to 18 months (Galloway et al. 1989).

Table 3-3 The Stages of Decomposition

Stage	State of the Remains
Initial Decay	– internal microorganisms active
	– gases produced internally
	– flesh intact and fresh in appearance
Putrefaction	– microbial activity intensified
	– body is bloated by internal gas
	– purge fluid leaks
	– odor of decay strong
Black Putrefaction	– gases and purge fluid escape as body collapses
	– odor of decay very strong
	– exposed flesh blackens
	– internal organs and tissues are of a creamy consistency
Butyric Fermentation	– exposed flesh fermenting
	– slow drying of tissue
	– flesh is a cheesy consistency
Dry Decay	– flesh is drying out and is hardening to a leathery texture
Skeletonization	– most of the soft tissue gone
	– bone is exposed
	– tendons, ligaments, and/or cartilage may still be intact
	– environmental factors will determine the process of decay in bone

Insect Activity

Insect activity affects the rate and process of decay, and modifies the condition of the remains. If the body is in an outdoor environment the odor of decaying flesh attracts a variety of **carrion** (*dead flesh eating*) insects. These insects scavenge and reproduce in many of the soft tissues and natural body openings, as well as in areas of flesh exposed by cuts or wounds. Insect activity accelerates decomposition and in certain environments, notably hot and humid ones, can reduce a body to bones within a week (Mann, Bass, and Meadows, 1990).

The variety and species of insects reproducing and feeding on fleshy remains depends entirely on the ecological area and the time of year. In warm climates where a body may be fully exposed, insect activity can begin before death even occurs, whereas in colder climates, there may be little to no insect activity.

Blow flies (*Calliphoridae*) and flesh flies (*Sarcophagidae*) are generally the most common type of insects at a death scene. The females lay their eggs or deposit larvae (maggots) in and around body orifices and open wounds. During their developmental stages they feed voraciously on the tissue. In doing so, they can skeletonize a full adult anywhere from four days in a hot, humid climate to weeks in a dry, cold environment.

Observing the level and stages of insect activity is most useful in estimating the time of death. Forensic entomologists (see chapter one) collect samples of the insects at the death scene in order to assess the time in which they or their eggs arrived. Since a variety of insects arrive on the body in succession during the process of decomposition and begin a predictable pattern of feeding and reproduction, entomologists assess the type and age of the insect and can associate this with the postmortem interval (Smith, 1986; Catts, 1990; Schoenly, 1992).

Table 3-4: Physical Variables Affecting the Decomposition Rate

Condition of Body	Decomposition Rate
small vs. large body size	– small bodies decompose at a faster rate than large bodies
whole vs. wounded/dismembered	– whole bodies decompose at a slower rate than wounded or dismembered parts
	– there are more tissues and openings available for microbial and insect infestation in the wounded/dismembered body, accelerating decay
nude vs. clothed and/or wrapped	– nude bodies decompose at a faster rate due to exposure to elements
	– heavy clothing, or wrapping around body slows rate of decomposition
contained and buried vs. not contained and buried	– contained and buried bodies decompose at a slower rate

*Adapted from Mann et al. (1990)

Table 3-5: Environmental Variables Affecting the Decomposition Rate

Environmental Variable	Decomposition Rate
cold climate	– decomposition rate is slowed and can be completely prevented if body is frozen
	– frozen bodies that are thawed decompose rapidly
	– cold, dry climate decay is slower than in cold, humid climate
	– decay is slower in cool, shaded areas
hot climate	– hot, humid weather accelerates decomposition
	– decomposition is slow in hot, dry climate
	– dry heat desiccates flesh, preserving skin and hair (mummification)
	– in direct sunlight dry decay is accelerated
moist and/or acidic soil	– decomposition rapid if body buried in these types of soil
sand, clay, and gravel soils with high pH (alkaline) levels	– decomposition is slower if body buried in these types of soil
presence of water	– bodies submerged in water will decompose slower than bodies on land, unless scavenged by aquatic organisms (fish, turtles, crustaceans)
	– decomposition is delayed in bodies submerged in very cold to freezing water
insect activity	– accelerates decomposition
animal/bird scavenging	– promotes and accelerates decomposition

*Adapted from Mann et al. (1990) and Galloway et al. (1989)

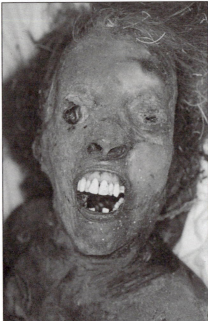

Fig. 3-5 (above). Maggot infestation (Photo, Courtesy of Jason H. Byrd).

Fig. 3-6 (left). Mummified human remains. Reprinted with permission, The Utah State Office of the Medical Examiner, all rights reserved.

Chapter Four

The Human Skeleton— A Beginner's Guide

The human skeleton is a highly vascular and complex system that performs numerous functions other than "holding up" the body. The skeletal system supports and protects soft tissues and vital organs while providing the levers and surfaces for the attachment of muscles, ligaments, and tendons. It is also the source of red blood cell production and the reserve of important minerals such as calcium and phosphorus. In addition, bones remove toxins and heavy metals, such as lead and arsenic, from the bloodstream.

Bone, in all higher vertebrates, is known for its hardness and resilience. Its tensile strength resembles cast iron without the weight and density; its flexibility resembles steel, and long after soft tissue has decomposed bone continues to endure. The reasons for such unique properties have to do with bone's structure and composition.

Living bone is made up of a blend of mostly inorganic components (calcium, phosphorus, magnesium, and small amounts of iron, sodium, and potassium), and organic substances (collagen fibers). Together these give living bone a hardness and elasticity that can withstand extreme weight and pressure. For example, a human adult femur can withstand 1800 to 2500 pounds of pressure before breaking. Nonliving bone is largely made up of the remaining hard, inorganic components which allow it to survive long after the decay of soft tissue. However, nonliving bone is more brittle, subject to easy splintering and breakage having lost its elastic, organic properties.

Structurally, bone varies according to its function and its position in the body. The *axial* skeleton, comprised of the skull, vertebrae, scapula, ribs, clavicle, sternum, and sacrum, is lightweight with greater flexibility and elasticity. These bones are generally flat and/or irregularly shaped, as they are related to breathing and the protection of vital organs. A typical bone from this region is made up of a thin shell of hard bone referred to as *compact bone*, surrounding layers of a spongy type bone called *cancellous bone*. This structural combination gives the axial skeleton lightness, without compromising its strength. Conversely, the *appendicular* skeleton, comprised of the bones of the arms, legs, and pelvis, is more heavyweight and durable. The bones in this part of the skeleton are designed to bear the weight and stress of grasping, holding, lifting, and constant locomotion. They are therefore made up of thicker layers of compact bone in a tubular structure surrounding cancellous bone. These bones can withstand enormous pressure and torsion while still being light enough to maneuver.

Fig. 4-1 A (right). The split
shaft of a tibia: (1) Cortical bone
surrounding a fine structure of
(2) cancellous bone

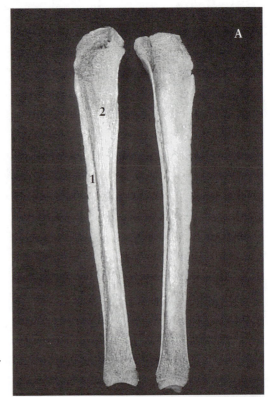

Fig. 4-1 B (below). A cross-section of bone from the cranium
(left) versus a cross-section of
long bone (right) displaying
differences in cortical bone thickness (Photos, John Doucette).

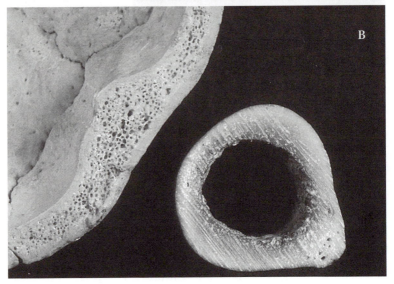

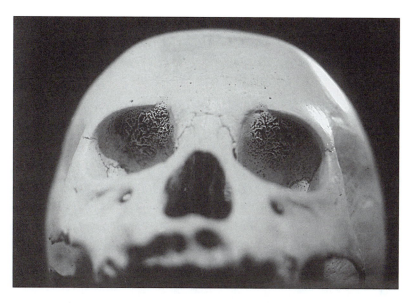

Fig. 4-2. Cribra Orbitalia, the porous appearance in the upper orbits, caused by iron deficiency anemia (Photo, Courtesy of the V. Doucette Collection).

The human adult skeleton accounts for approximately 15 percent of overall body weight and along with cartilage forms the dense connective tissue of the body. The average adult human has 206 bones, however this number often varies due to the presence, in some individuals and populations, of what are known as *supernumerary* bones. These extra bones are often very small, located in the hands and feet, and are between muscles or tendons, rather than actual sites for muscle attachment. Their number, size, and shape are unpredictable and are therefore not categorized.

The fetal and subadult skeletons have more than 300 bones, as individual bones are in separate parts during their growth and development. Eventually these parts fuse to become one bone (see Chapter 5). The number of bones thus varies according to age.

Though living bone is made up of mostly inorganic substances, it is a dynamic tissue that is capable of responding to a wide variety of physical and environmental stimuli. As such, it is in a constant state of change. The types of changes to living bone, are referred to as modeling, which occurs from approximately the third intrauterine month to the age of approximately 25-30 years, and remodeling which takes place throughout an individual's life.

Modeling takes place when bone cells size and shape the fetal and subadult skeleton from the point at which physical growth begins through to maturity (Frost, 1985). Although genetics play a large part in determining the overall size and shape of an individual's bones, there are other factors which may interfere with the normal processes of growth and development, such as nutritional deficiencies, disease, and medication. For example, deficiencies in vitamin C and D during childhood can lead to diseases such as scurvy and rickets both of which affect bone density and cause bone to atrophy (Stuart-Macadam, 1989:201-222).

Remodeling involves the same kind of bone cell activity as modeling, but it is an ongoing event separate from the processes of growth and development. Although bone in the adult skeleton has stopped growing, its density, shape and size can still change in response to factors such as aging, exercise, injury, trauma, disease, diet, and occupational stress (Frost, 1985; Kennedy, 1989). The degree to which these changes occur depend on the intensity and the duration of the factors listed above. Terms such as "dog-walker's elbow," "weaver's bottom," "snowmobiler's back," "milker's neck," all describe the sorts of modification of various parts of the skeleton brought about by an individual's occupation or hobby (Kennedy, 1989:129-160).

Over time, the results of both modeling and remodeling present a record of events much like the pattern of tree rings which reveal instances of growth, disease, and environmental change by their size and shape. Unlike other tissues of the body, the bumps, grooves, stress lines, healed fractures, or breaks in bone provide a record of past events, lifestyle habits, and occupational stress. Such information is vital when assessing human remains for the purpose of identification.

While a good understanding of the skeletal system is important in forensic anthropology, a thorough knowledge of the *morphology* (shape) and characteristics that distinguish skeletal parts is essential. Having in mind a good visual image of each bone allows one to identify and differentiate its numerous qualities. This skill is vital especially when one is faced with fragmented, cut, burned, or commingled skeletal remains.

The following is an inventory of the skeletal system with a summary and brief description of each part. Along with these are photographs labeled with the anatomical names associated with each bone for easy reference.

Table 4-1

Common Name	Anatomical Term	Number of Bones	Description
Skull	Calvarium		Bones that form the vault and cranial cavity accommodating the brain
	Frontal	1	
	Parietal	2	
	Occipital	1	
	Sphenoid	1	
	Ethmoid	1	
	Temporal	2	
	contains:		
	Malleus	2	Ear Ossicles (bones of hearing). All 3 are in each ear
	Incus	2	
	Stapes	2	
	Facial Skeleton		Parts of the skull that form the face
	Nasal	2	Forms the bridge of the nose
	Vomer	1	Divides the nasal cavity into left and right sides
	Turbinate bones	2	Thin scroll of bone in nasal cavity
	Lacrimal	2	Small, thin bones of the eye socket
	Zygomatic	2	The cheek bones
	Maxilla	2	The upper jaw
	Palatine	2	The roof of the mouth
Lower Jaw	Mandible	1	Bears the lower teeth and forms joint with the skull
	Hyoid	1	Small u-shaped bone located just beneath the lower jaw in the neck region
Backbone	Vertebrae	33 (total)	Vertebrae are divided into types according to their location:
	cervical	7	Located in the neck region
	thoracic	12	Located in the trunk region. Articulate with ribs to form rib cage
	lumbar	5	Located in the lower back
	sacral	5	Fused together to form the sacrum
	coccygeal	4	Very small vertebrae fused together to form the coccyx, or "tailbone"

Common Name	Anatomical Term	Number of Bones	Description
Chest	Thoracic Cage	12 ribs	The cage is formed by 12 ribs articulated to the vertebrae of the back and the sternum in front
	Sternum, composed of:		
	manubrium	1	Uppermost part of the breastbone that articulates with the first rib and the clavicle
	body	4 fused bones	Fused sternebrae form the body and articulate with ribs 2 to 7
	xiphoid process	1	The lowest part of the sternum
Shoulder Blade	Scapula	2 (paired)	Located on the back of the thoracic cage Articulates with the head of the humerus and the clavicle
Collar Bone	Clavicle	2 (paired)	S-shaped strut that holds the shoulders back Articulates with the sternum and the scapula
Upper arm	Humerus	2 (paired)	Extends from the shoulder to elbow and articulates with the scapula as a socket, and below with the radius and ulna
Forearm	Radius	2 (paired)	Located laterally (thumb-side) and articulates above (proximally) with the humerus, and side to side with the ulna
	Ulna	2 (paired)	Upper part forms a hinge joint with the humerus to form the elbow
			Articulates side to side with the radius
Wrist	Carpals	16 (8 in each wrist)	Irregularly shaped bones arranged in two rows (proximal and distal) to form the wrist bones
	trapezium		
	trapezoid		
	capitate		
	hamate		
	scaphoid		
	lunate		
	triquetral		
	pisiform		

Common Name	Anatomical Term	Number of Bones	Description
Hand	*Metacarpals*	10	5 in each hand
Fingers	*Phalanges*	28	3 in each finger and 2 in each thumb (14 for each hand)
Hip Bone	*Innominate Bone,* composed of:	2 (paired)	The innominate, formed by the fused ilium, ischium and pubis, is paired, and articulates with the sacrum to form the basin-shaped pelvis
	ilium	fused	
	ischium		
	pubis		
Thigh	*Femur*	2 (paired)	The bone of the thigh articulates with the acetabulum, a cup-shaped socket on each innominate, and with the tibia at the knee It is the longest and largest bone of the skeleton
Knee Cap	*Patella*	2 (paired)	A round-shaped, flat bone within the tendon, at the distal end of the femur
Shin and Lower Leg	*Tibia*	2 (paired)	The larger bone of the lower leg articulates proximally with the femur at the knee, and forms the inner (medial) ankle at its distal end
	Fibula	2 (paired)	The thin bone of the lower leg lateral to the tibia forms the outer (lateral) ankle
Ankle and Heel	*Tarsals*		
	talus	2 (paired)	Articulates with the tibia and fibula, and rests on the calcaneus. The talus provides the ankle movements of flexion and extension
	calcaneus	2 (paired)	The largest of the tarsal bones forms the heel of the foot and supports the talus
	navicular	2 (paired)	A boat-shaped bone that articulates with the 3 cuneiform bones to form the elevated arch of the foot
	cuboid	2 (paired)	The most lateral (side) bone of the tarsals
	3 cuneiforms (lateral, medial & intermediate)	2 of each (paired)	With the navicular bone these wedge-shaped bones form the elevated arch of the foot

Common Name	Anatomical Term	Number of Bones	Description
Foot	*Metatarsals*	10	5 in each foot
Toes	*Phalanges*	28	2 phalanges for the first toe and 3 for each of the other toes (14 for each foot)

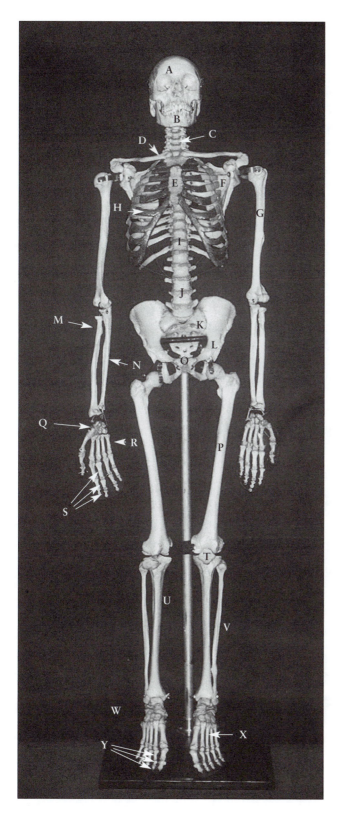

Fig. 4-3.
The Human Skeleton.

A. Cranium

B. Mandible

C. Cervical vertebrae

D. Clavicle

E. Sternum

F. Scapula

G. Humerus

H. Ribs

I. Thoracic vertebrae

J. Lumbar vertebrae

K. Sacrum

L. Innominate (coxa)

M. Radius

N. Ulna

O. Coccyx

P. Femur

Q. Carpal bones

R. Metacarpals

S. Phalanges

T. Patella

U. Tibia

V. Fibula

W. Tarsal bones

X. Metatarsals

Y. Phalanges

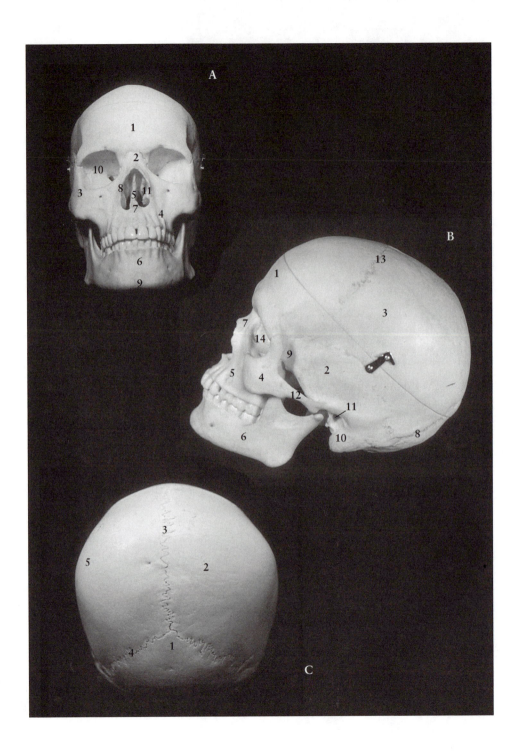

Fig. 4-4. The Skull.

A. (top left) Frontal view.

    1.   Frontal bone
    2.   Nasal bone
    3.   Zygomatic bone
    4.   Maxilla
    5.   Vomer
    6.   Mandible
    7.   Anterior nasal spine
    8.   Nasal aperture
    9.   Mental protuberance
    10. Sphenoid bone (greater wing)
    11. Nasal concha

B. (center right) Lateral view

    1.   Frontal bone
    2.   Temporal bone
    3.   Parietal bone
    4.   Zygomatic bone
    5.   Maxilla
    6.   Mandible
    7.   Nasal bone
    8.   Occipital bone
    9.   Sphenoid
    10. Mastoid process
    11. External auditory meatus
    12. Zygomatic arch
    13. Coronal suture
    14. Lacrimal bone

C. (bottom left) Occipital view./

    1.   Occipital bone
    2.   Parietal bone
    3.   Sagittal suture
    4.   Lambdoidal suture
    5.   Parietal eminence

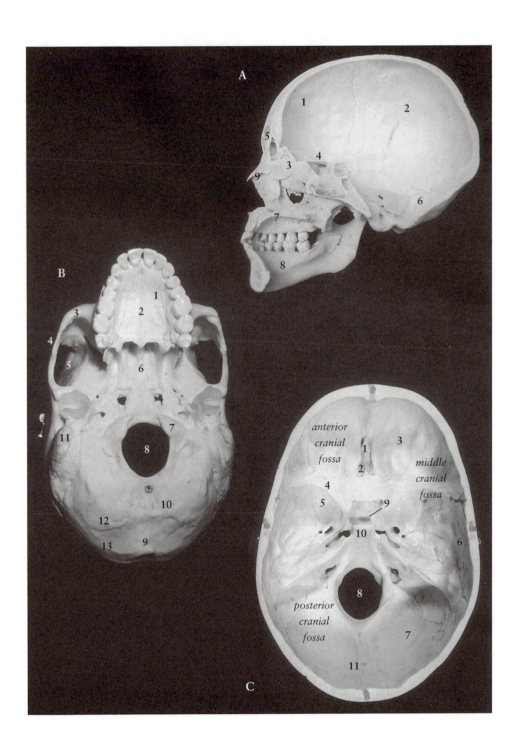

Fig. 4-4. The Skull (cont.).

A. (top right) Interior view, sagittal cross-section.

1. Frontal bone
2. Parietal bone
3. Ethmoid bone
4. Sphenoid bone (lesser wing)
5. Frontal sinus
6. Occipital bone
7. Maxilla
8. Mandible
9. Nasal bone

B. (center left) Basilar view.

1. Palate
2. Median palatine suture
3. Zygomatic bone
4. Zygomatic arch
5. Temporal bone
6. Vomer
7. Occipital condyle
8. Foramen magnum
9. External occipital protuberance
10. Occipital bone
11. Mastoid process
12. Inferior nuchal line
13. Superior nuchal line

C. (bottom right) Interior view of the base.

1. Crista galli
2. Cribiform plate of ethmoid bone
3. Orbital part of frontal bone
4. Sphenoid bone (lesser wing)
5. Sphenoid bone (greater wing)
6. Temporal bone (squamous part)
7. Occipital bone
8. Foramen magnum
9. Hypophyseal fossa
10. Dorsum sellae
11. Internal occipital protuberance

Fig. 4-5. The Sphenoid, anterior view.

1. Lesser wing
2. Greater wing
3. Sphenoidal sinus
4. Sphenoidal crest
5. Pterygoid process

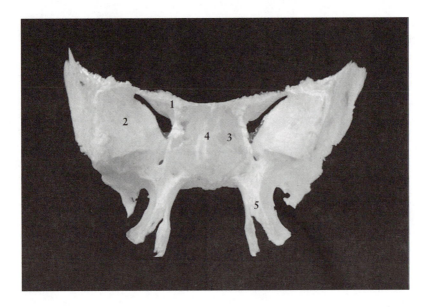

Fig. 4-6. The Bones of the Ear: A – Stapes; B – Incus; and C – Malleus.

1. Head of the stapes
2. Base of the stapes
3. Short crus of the incus
4. Facet for malleus
5. Long crus of the incus
6. Head of the malleus
7. Posterior spur of the malleus
8. Manubrium of the malleus

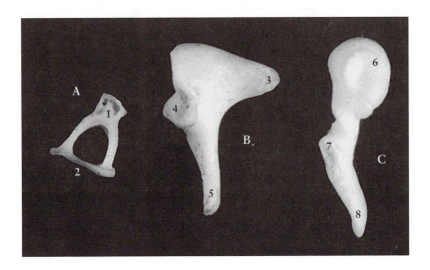

Fig. 4-7. The Mandible.

1. Body
2. Ramus
3. Gonial angle
4. Coronoid process
5. Head (condyle)
6. Madibular notch
7. Mental foramen
8. Mental protuberance
9. Alveolar border

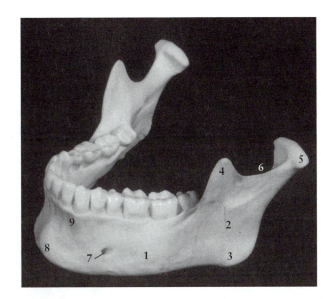

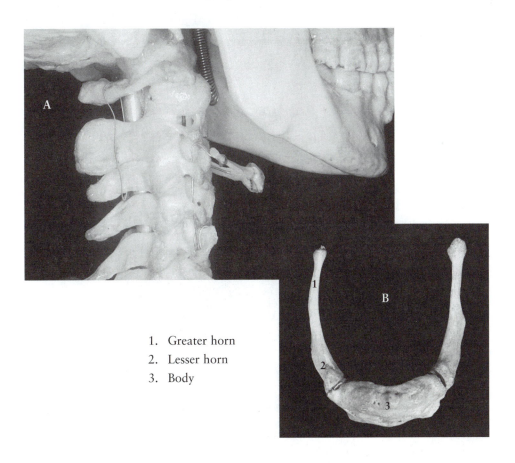

1. Greater horn
2. Lesser horn
3. Body

Fig. 4-8. The Hyoid Bone: A – Lateral view and B – Superior view.

Fig. 4-9. The Verebral Column

A. Cervical vertebrae

B. Thoracic vertebrae

C. Lumbar vertebrae

D. Sacrum

E. Coccyx

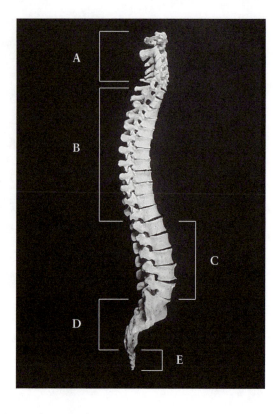

Fig. 4-10. (below) Typical vertebrae, superior view.

A. Cervical vertebrae.

1. Body
2. Transverse process
3. Spinous process
4. Transverse foramen
5. Superior articular facet
6. Vertebral foramen

B. Thoracic vertebrae

1. Body
2. Pedicle
3. Transverse process
4. Superior articular process
5. Spinous process
6. Vertebral foramen

C. Lumbar vertebrae

1. Body
2. Pedicle
3. Costal process
4. Superior articular process
5. Spinous process
6. Vertebral foramen
7. Mamillary process

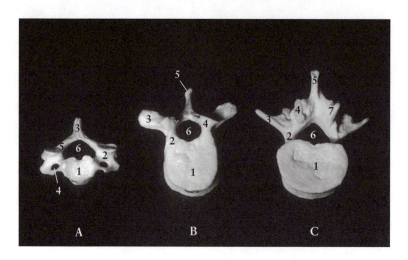

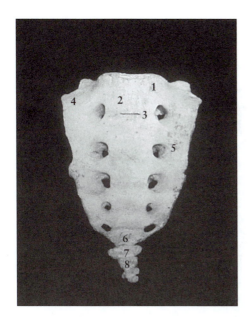

Fig. 4-11. The Sacrum and Coccyx, ventral view.

1. Sacral promontory
2. Body of the first sacral vertebra
3. First transverse line
4. Ala (lateral part)
5. Second pelvic sacral foramen
6. Apex
7. First coccygeal vertebra
8. Fused second to fourth vertebrae

Fig. 4-12. Detail of Coccyx, dorsal view.

1. Coccygeal horn
2. Transverse process
3. First coccygeal vertebra
4. Fused second to fourth vertebrae

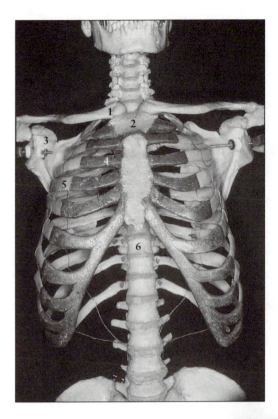

Fig. 4-13 A. (left) The Thorax: The Chest and Shoulder Girdle, ventral view.

1. Clavicle
2. Sternum
3. Scapula
4. Costal cartilage
5. Ribs I–XII
6. Thoracic vertebrae

Fig. 4-13 B. (right) The Thorax: The Chest and Shoulder Girdle, dorsal view.

1. Clavicle
2. Scapula
3. Ribs I–XII
4. Thoracic vertebrae

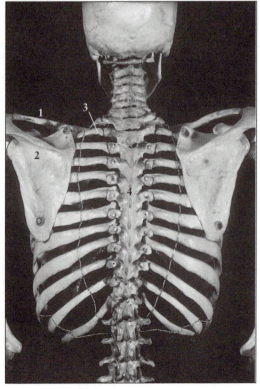

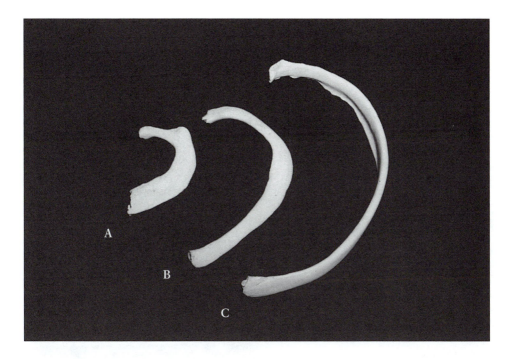

Fig. 4-14. (above) A comparative view of ribs: A – The first rib (Rib I); B – The second rib (Rib II); and C – A central rib.

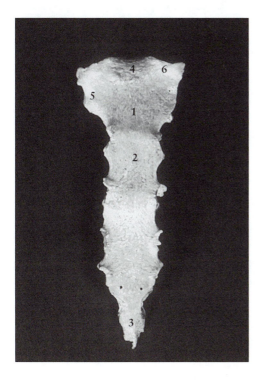

Fig. 4-15. (left) The Sternum, anterior view.

1. Manubrium
2. Body
3. Xiphoid process
4. Jugular notch
5. Notch for first costal cartilage
6. Clavicular notch

Fig. 4-16. The Scapula

A. Left dorsal view

1.   Acromion
2.   Spine
3.   Supraspinous fossa
4.   Superior angle
5.   Infraspinous fossa
6.   Medial border
7.   Inferior angle
8.   Lateral border

B. Left ventral view

1.   Coracoid process
2.   Neck
3.   Glenoid cavity
4.   Superior angle
5.   Subscapular fossa
6.   Medial border
7.   Inferior angle
8.   Lateral border

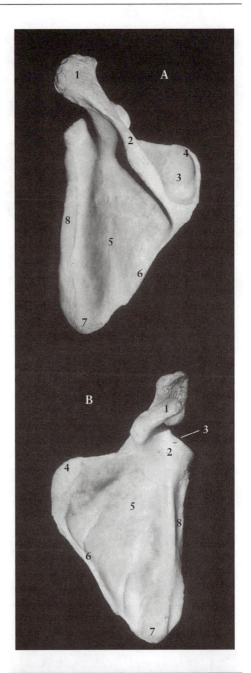

**Fig. 4-17. The Clavicle,
left inferior view.**

1.   Sternal facet
2.   Costal tuberosity
3.   Groove for subclavius muscle
4.   Conoid tubercle
5.   Acromial facet

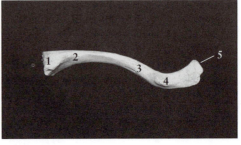

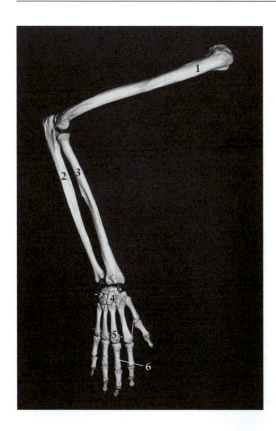

Fig. 4-18. The Articulated Bones of the Arm, right dorsal view.

1. Humerus
2. Ulna
3. Radius
4. Carpals
5. Metacarpals
6. Phalanges

Fig. 4-19. The Radius.

A. Left ventral view

1. Head
2. Neck
3. Radial tuberosity
4. Interosseous margin
5. Styloid process

B. Right dorsal view

1. Head
2. Dorsal tubercle

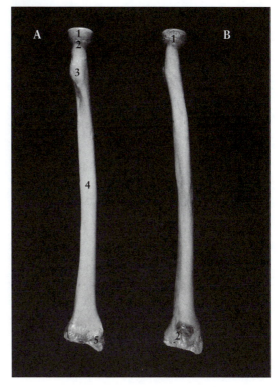

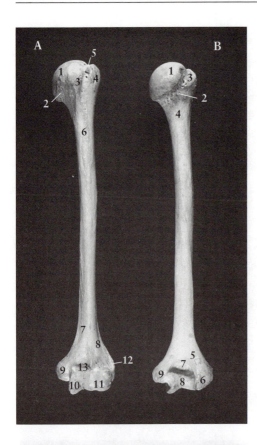

Fig. 4-20. The Humerus.

A. Left ventral view

1.   Head
2.   Anatomical neck
3.   Lesser tuberosity
4.   Greater tuberosity
5.   Intertubercular groove
6.   Surgical neck
7.   Medial epicondylar ridge
8.   Lateral epicondylar ridge
9.   Medial epicondyle
10. Trochlea
11. Capitulum
12. Lateral epicondyle
13. Coronoid fossa

B. Right dorsal view

1.   Head
2.   Anatomical neck
3.   Greater tuberosity
4.   Surgical neck
5.   Lateral supracondylar ridge
6.   Lateral epicondyle
7.   Olecranon fossa
8.   Trochlea
9.   Medial epicondyle

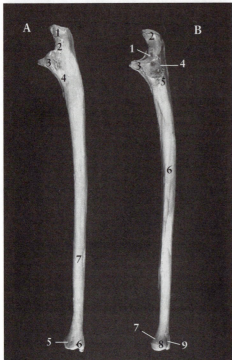

Fig. 4-21. The Ulna.

A. Right ventral view

1.   Olecranon process
2.   Trochlear notch
3.   Coronoid process
4.   Tuberosity
5.   Head
6.   Styloid process
7.   Medial surface

B. Left lateral view

1.   Trochlear notch
2.   Olecranon process
3.   Coronoid process
4.   Radial notch
5.   Supinator crest
6.   Interosseous margin
7.   Head
8.   Extensor carpi ulnaris groove
9.   Styloid process

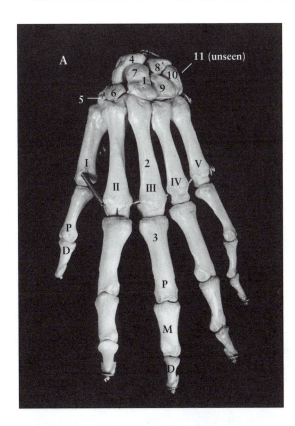

Fig. 4-22. The Articulated Bones of the Hand.

A. Left dorsal view

1. The eight bones of the wrist (carpals), see 4–11
2. The metacarpals, I–V
3. The phalanges: proximal (P), middle (M), and distal (D)
4. Scaphoid
5. Trapezium
6. Trapezoid
7. Capitate
8. Lunate
9. Hamate
10. Triquetral
11. Pisiform

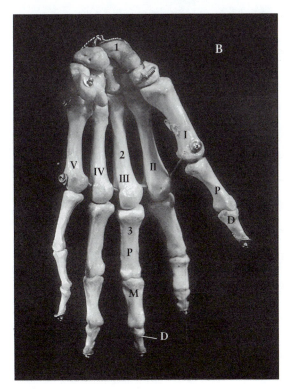

B. Left palmar view

1. The eight bones of the wrist (carpals) (*see dorsal view, A.4–A.11 above*)
2. The metacarpals, I–V
3. The phalanges: proximal (P), middle (M) and distal (D)

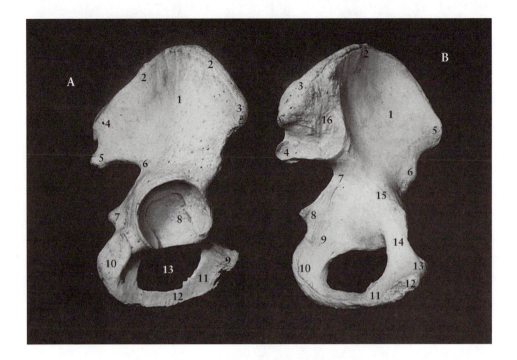

Fig. 4-23. The Innominate (os coxa).

A. Right lateral view

1. Anterior gluteal line
2. Iliac crest
3. Anterior superior iliac spine
4. Posterior superior iliac spine
5. Posterior inferior iliac spine
6. Greater sciatic notch
7. Ischial spine
8. Acetabulum
9. Pubic tubercle
10. Ischial tuberosity
11. Body of pubis
12. Inferior ramus of pubis
13. Obturator foramen

B. Left medial view

1. Iliac fossa
2. Iliac crest
3. Iliac tuberosity
4. Posterior inferior iliac spine
5. Anterior superior iliac spine
6. Anterior inferior iliac spine
7. Greater sciatic notch
8. Ischial spine
9. Body of ischium
10. Ischial tuberosity
11. Ischiopubic ramus
12. Pubic crest
13. Pubic tubercle
14. Superior ramus of pubis
15. Arcuate line
16. Auricular surface

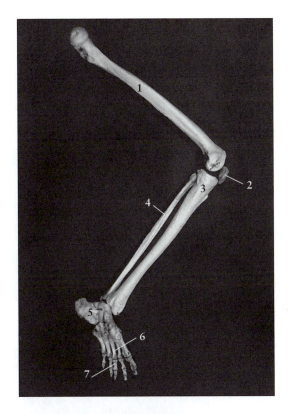

Fig. 4-24. The Articulated Bones of the Leg, left medial view.

1. Femur
2. Patella
3. Tibia
4. Fibula
5. Tarsal bones
6. Metatarsals, I–V
7. Phalanges

Fig. 4-25. The Patella.

A. Right anterior view

1. Base
2. Apex

B. Left posterior view

1. Lateral facet
2. Medial facet

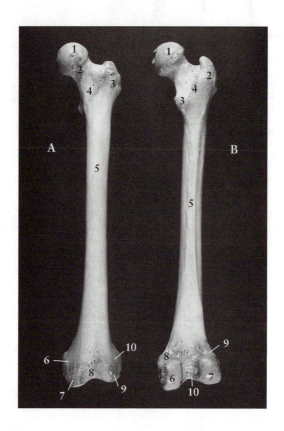

Fig. 4-26. The Femur.

A. Left ventral view

1. Head
2. Neck
3. Greater trochanter
4. Intertrochanteric line
5. Shaft
6. Medial epicondyle
7. Medial condyle
8. Patellar surface
9. Lateral condyle
10. Lateral epicondyle

B. Right dorsal view

1. Head
2. Greater trochanter
3. Lesser trochanter
4. Intertrochanteric crest
5. Linea aspera
6. Medial condyle
7. Lateral condyle
8. Medial epicondyle
9. Lateral epicondyle
10. Intercondylar fossa

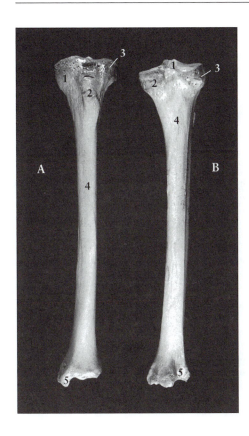

Fig. 4-27. The Tibia.

A. Left ventral view

1. Medial condyle
2. Tibial tuberosity
3. Lateral condyle
4. Anterior margin
5. Medial malleolus

B. Right dorsal view

1. Tubercles of interdondylar eminence
2. Medial condyle
3. Lateral condyle
4. Posterior surface
5. Fibular notch

Fig. 4-28. The Fibula.

A. Left lateral view

1. Apex of head
2. Head
3. Shaft
4. Lateral surface
5. Lateral malleolus

B. Right medial view

1. Apex of head
2. Articular surface of head
3. Interosseous margin
4. Articular surface for talus
5. Lateral malleolar fossa

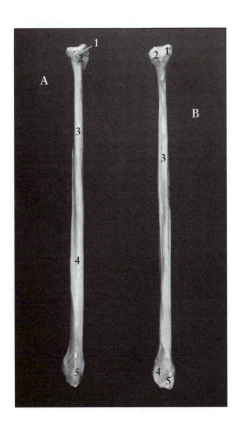

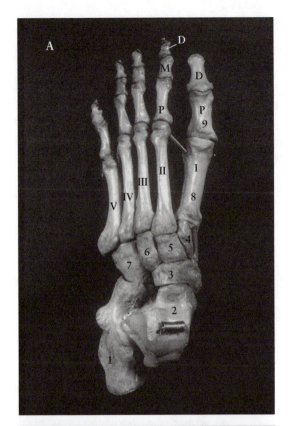

Fig. 4-29. The Articulated Bones of the Foot.

A. Left dorsal view

1. Calcaneus
2. Talus
3. Navicular
4. Medial cuneiform
5. Intermediate cuneiform
6. Lateral cuneiform
7. Cuboid
8. Metatarsals, I–V
9. The phalanges:
   proximal (P), middle (M)
   and distal (D)

(*A.1-7 are tarsal bones*)

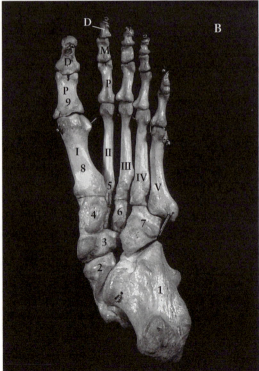

B. Left plantar view

1. Calcaneus
2. Talus
3. Navicular
4. Medial cuneiform
5. Intermediate cuneiform
6. Lateral cuneiform
7. Cuboid
8. Metatarsals, I–V
9. The phalanges:
   proximal (P), middle (M)
   and distal (D)

(*B.1-7 are tarsal bones*)

Fig. 30. A Comparison of Animal bones.

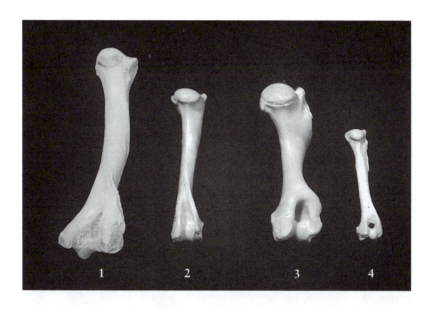

A. The humerus of a (1) bear; (2) deer, (3) pig, and (4) dog.

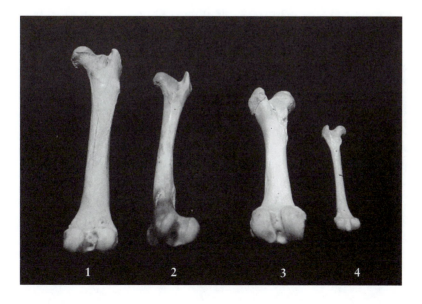

B. The femur of a (1) bear; (2) deer, (3) pig, and (4) dog.

Fig. 30. (cont.)

C. The tibia of a (1) bear; (2) deer, (3) pig, and (4) dog (with attached fibula).

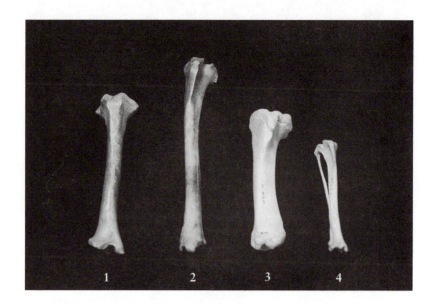

Fig. 4-31. The Metacarpals and Proximal Phalanges of a Bear (Metalcarpals II–V).

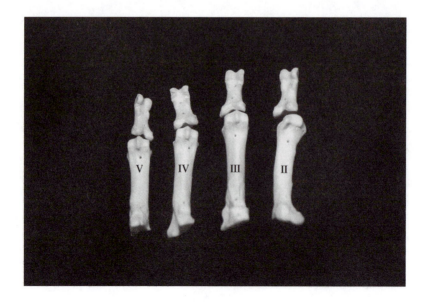

Section III

Uncovering the Mystery

Chapter Five

Assessing the Remains

Chapter five provides a general description of some of the more popular identification methods currently used by forensic anthropologists when assessing human remains. The chapter is divided into sections according to the category of identification and the methods applied for each. An overview of the development of these identification methods follows this introduction and is intended to provide a context from which to view their application.

Introduction to Identification Techniques

Biological Identity

It is assumed that once an individual's facial features, hair, soft tissue, and muscles have decomposed, an "identity" is no longer apparent. In one sense this is true. Positively identifying an individual, that is, by their name and their date and place of birth is not possible by simply examining their skeletal remains. However, an individual's biological identity is not altogether lost with the fleshy parts. Traits that characterize sex, age, race, and stature leave their mark on bone and are evident long after an individual's death.

The assessment methods used by forensic anthropologists for determining a biological identity involve both direct observation and the taking of measurements. Certain features, marked by shape and size on the skeleton are examined, noted, and compared. Some of these features are genetic in nature; others have been shaped or modified by factors such as diet, illness, disease, and/or trauma.

In assessing these features for identification purposes, the forensic anthropologist attempts to narrow the range of possible persons down to a smaller subsection of the population that is less numerous. They must ultimately demonstrate the likelihood that the individual is someone from a specific population, like a six-foot-two, 25-year-old caucasian male, for example. As the range within a specific population becomes more narrow, the possibility of a positive identification becomes greater. Otherwise, unidentified skeletal remains derived from a nonspecific population simply amount to any number of possible biological identities.

Morphological vs. Metric Analysis

Most of the assessment methods outlined in this chapter involve the observation of features, marked by shape and size, on the skeleton. This way of examin-

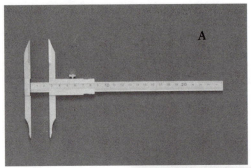

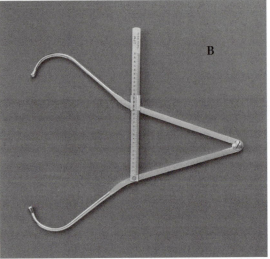

Fig. 5-1. A–Sliding Caliper, measures the distance between two points; B–Spreading Caliper, used for measuring the distance between landmarks on opposite sides of the skull (Photos, Courtesy of SiberHegner, Zurich).

ing skeletal material is referred to as a ***morphological*** analysis. Familiarity with and knowledge of skeletal variation within and between various populations is key to the successful application of morphological methods. In other words, forensic anthropologists must be able to differentiate the sorts of traits that distinguish one individual from the next within that individual's own population, and those that distinguish them from others in another population altogether.

Other methods of assessing remains require one to take extensive measurements and compare them to the recorded measurements of known samples. This approach is referred to as a ***metric*** analysis. In applying metric methods, one enters the realm of statistics. Like most physical anthropologists, forensic anthropologists encounter statistics when conducting and interpreting their research. Assigning a biological identity to human skeletal remains entails an understanding of what metric methods to apply and the mathematical probability of their error. For any individual not versed in statistical terms or procedures, the information and application can be confusing. Hence, metric methods will be noted briefly in this chapter. For a more thorough treatment of metric methods one can refer to: Steele & Bramblett, 1988; İşcan & Kennedy, 1989; Ferembach et al., 1980.

Skeletal Collections

Documented skeletal collections have always been essential to forensic anthropologists as the primary, if not only, source used to derive estimates of sex, age, race, and stature. Observing and measuring the skeletons of known individuals from a particular collection was a means by which inferences were made about the larger living population. Early collections were made up of hundreds of dissecting room cadavers from university hospitals across the United States, unclaimed bodies from morgues, as well as American casualties from World War II and the Korean War. Most of the individuals in the collection are adult whites, blacks, and Native Americans of known identity, born in the late 19th and early 20th centuries. Some of the more popular collections studied by anthropologists through the years include the *Hamann-Todd Collection* at the Cleveland Museum of Natural History, composed of 3,100 skeletons (the largest one in the world), the *Terry Collection*, composed of 1,600 skeletons housed in the Smithsonian Institute, and the *Cobb Collection* of 600 skeletons at Howard University in Washington, D.C.

From their extensive measuring, observing, and documenting of various parts and traits on the skeletons in these collections, anthropologists were able to establish measurement tools and standards. The most popular of these include the stature estimation formulae used to estimate height (Trotter & Gleser, 1952), the race and sex cranial discriminant functions for determining an individual's race and sex (Giles & Elliot, 1962), and various aging methods (Todd, 1920; McKern and Stewart, 1957; Lovejoy et al., 1985b).

The measurement tools and standards were designed to be applied to unknown skeletal remains. Unfortunately, the early collections are comprised of many elderly individuals and very few females, which create immediate biases in

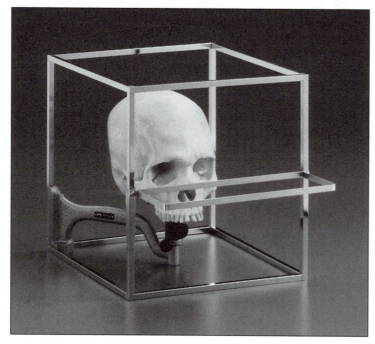

Fig. 5-2A. Measuring the cranium with a cubic craniophor (Photos, Courtesy of SiberHegner, Zurich).

Fig. 5-2B.
Mandibulometer,
measures the height,
angle and width of
the mandible (Photos,
Courtesy of SiberHeg-
ner, Zurich).

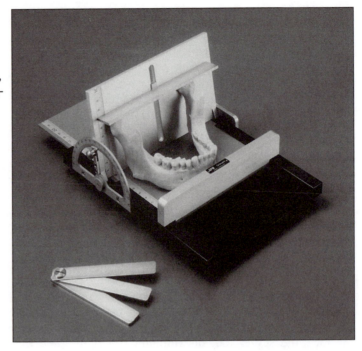

the data. Applying standards derived from these collections to modern skeletal remains becomes problematic, especially since the population of North America is far more genetically and demographically varied than it was at the turn of the last century. As such, many anthropologists have questioned the use of some of the traditional assessment methods listed above, and have demonstrated instances of misclassification when these methods and standards were applied to forensic cases (Erickson, 1982; Ayers et al., 1989; Meadows & Jantz, 1995; Ousley, 1995).

The Forensic Data Bank

Currently, there are very few modern skeletal collections from which to derive new standards that truly reflect the genetic and demographic variation of North America. To deal with this void of information, a modern forensic database, the Forensic Data Bank (FDB) was established at the University of Tennessee, Knoxville, in the late 1980s. The FDB is an ongoing collection of metric and non-metric reference data derived from modern skeletons, mostly forensic cases, contributed in large part by forensic anthropologists across North America. Information on various cases with known identities can be accessed for comparative and research purposes. The Bank's data can also be used for the testing of methods of sex, age and race determination, and as a foundation for new techniques (Ousley & Jantz, 1998.).

Hopefully, with cooperation from the forensic community and consistent data collection, the FDB will continue to establish more suitable standards and methods for the purpose of identifying increasingly varied skeletal remains.

Methods of Biological Identification

Sex Determination

Sexual Dimorphism

Sexual differences develop prenatally and become more marked through infancy and adolescence. Where the growth processes for males and females are the same, the onset and duration of puberty differ. Females begin puberty and end it more quickly whereas males begin and end it at a later age. This results in what is referred to as *sexual dimorphism*, the differences in size and shape that exist between males and females within a population.

In human populations, overall size differences between the sexes are small, but the amount of sexual dimorphism will vary from population to population. Experience with dimorphic traits particular to a population increases ones understanding of the dimorphism in that population only. There is a potential for great error if these known traits are then applied to unknown individuals from different populations. One risks the chance of misidentifying for example, a large female from one sample for a male from another. Also, characteristics that distinguish human races can be confused with sex differences.

Attributing sex to unidentified remains early on is an important requirement as many of the additional identity methods, like age and stature estimation, are sex-specific. These are discussed in more detail below.

Sex Determination in the Adult vs. the Immature Skeleton

The marked appearance of sexual dimorphic traits on bone are directly related to the age of an individual. The presence of secondary sexual characteristics, for example, the widening of hips in females, robusticity in males, is controlled hormonally and mark the onset of puberty at a particular age. Therefore, the indication of sex is most readily apparent in the adult skeleton, specifically in the pelvis and skull. The assignment of sex to the prepubescent skeleton is more difficult than in the adult skeleton due to the absence of these secondary sexual characteristics. As well, immature skeletons are incomplete as most of the bones have not yet reached their full growth potential. The opposite, however is true, in that aging the subadult skeleton is easier than in the adult skeleton (see Age Determination, below) Hence, in assigning a sex to the subadult skeleton, methods other than those involving the assessment of the pelvis and skull are considered.

One method was proposed of sexing the subadult skeleton by comparing the stage of dental calcification with the stage of maturation of the post-cranial skeleton (Hunt and Gleiser 1955). The rates of dental development for males and females are relatively the same, whereas their post-cranial development differ. Generally, female skeletons mature at a faster rate than male skeletons. Apparently by assessing the dental age and the individual's post-cranial age and then comparing these to the known standards, it is possible to estimate sex. If the dental age and the post-cranial age do not agree, then the individual is most likely female. If they do agree, the individual is most likely male. Unfortunately it has been difficult to prove the reliability of this method due to the variation that ex-

.ists in post-cranial development within different populations. Therefore, it is not a popular method for use in forensic cases.

Most often, if an immature skeleton is discovered, investigators look for other clues that may indicate whether the individual was male or female. Premortem dental records of known individuals for a specific age set are used to compare with the dental remains. Ideally, if the remains still contain scalp hair, accessories, bits of clothing, or jewelry, these are used to compare with the information provided by the next of kin.

Sexing techniques involve morphological and metric analyses of the remains. The methods briefly outlined in this section are largely morphological and are intended for the adult skeleton. For metric methods in sex determination, one may refer to: Giles and Elliot, 1963; Brothwell, 1981; Steele and Bramblett, 1988.

General Traits of the Pelvis

The bones of the adult pelvis provide an abundant source of information in the determination of sex, but in the rare event that an entire skeleton is available for assessment, other bones should be used for analysis, especially the skull and long bones. Measurement of the long bones is necessary, if they are available, but without the pelvis they are less accurate as reliable indicators.

The sacrum and two innominate bones form the pelvis. The innominate bone (known also as the *os coxa*) is made up of three fused bones, the *ilium,* the *ischium* and the *pubis.* In females, the pelvic inlet (superior and inferior aperture) is broad, rounder, and generally wider with a large interior diameter and a wide subpubic angle designed to accommodate fetal development and birth. In males, the pelvis is generally higher and more narrow, with the pelvic outlet obstructed by a curved sacrum and coccyx, as well as a narrow subpubic angle creating a heart-shaped superior aperture.

Table 5-1 below outlines the size and shape differences apparent between the male and female innominate bones which are only applicable to late adolescents and adults.

Table 5-1. General Differences Between the Male and Female Pelvis

Trait	Male	Female
Iliac Blades	high, not flared	flared laterally
Greater Sciatic Notch	constricted, approx. 30° angle	wide, approx. 60° angle
Preauricular Sulcus	shallow if present	deep, if present
Acetabulum	larger, deep	small, shallow
Subpubic Angle	acute	obtuse
Pubis	short	long
Ventral Arc	ridge not present	ridge is present
Subpubic Concavity	slight depression, or absent	large concavity

*Modified from Brothwell, 1981 and Ubelaker, 1978.

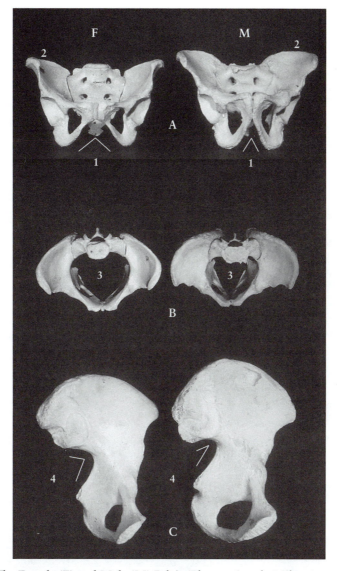

Fig. 5-3. The Female (F) and Male (M) Pelvis (Photos, Angela Milana).

A. Ventral view (top row)

  1. Subpubic angle is obtuse in females (<90°) and acute in males (>90°).

  2. Iliac blades are flared more laterally in females and are higher in males.

B. Superior view (middle row)

  3. The pelvic aperture is wide and round in females, narrow and heart-shaped in males.

C. Internal view (bottom row)

  4. Greater sciatic notch is wider in females, +60° angle. In males it is constricted to approximately a 30° angle.

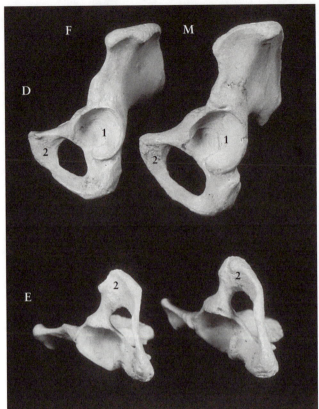

Fig. 5-3. (cont.) The Female (F) and Male (M) Pelvis (Photos, Angela Milana).

D. Ventral view (top row)

1. The acetabulum appears larger and deeper in males.

E. Inferior view (bottom row)

2. The body of the pubis is broader and more rectangular in females.

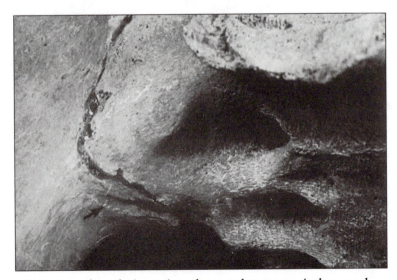

Fig. 5-4. The arrow, where the innominate bone and sacrum articulate, marks a groove known as the preauricular sulcus, indicating that this individual had given birth (Photo, John Doucette).

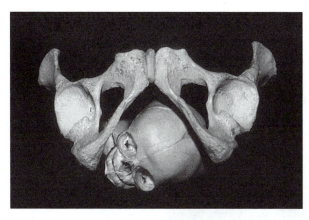

Fig. 5-5. The fetal skull is positioned to illustrate the biological necessity for a wide subpubic angle and inferior aperture in the female pelvis (Photo, Angela Milana).

General Traits in the Skull

Estimation of sex from a morphological and metric assessment of the skull is based on the same generalization that males are more robust (larger) and taller than females in adult populations, although as stated earlier, the size differences for each population varies considerably.

Cranial areas, like the postcranial, show sexual dimorphic differences (see Table 5-2), manifested by more massive areas of muscle insertion and origin in males than in females. Generally, the female skull retains more gracility and smoothness, characteristic of prepubescent cranium, with thinner less prominent ridges and crests. Male skulls are relatively larger and more robust with rougher surface areas. These differences when skulls are compared, are most prominent around the chin and jaw (*gonial angles*), the back of the head (*occipital protuberance* and *nuchal crest*), the cheekbones (*zygomatic arch* and *bones*), the brow ridges above the eye sockets (*supraorbital ridges*), and the forehead (*frontal bone*).

Table 5-2. Differences between the Male and Female Skull

Trait	Male	Female
Frontal Bone	steep, rugged	rounded, smooth
Supraorbital Ridge	prominent, large	smooth, gracile, sharp border
Orbits	squared, blunt superior margins	rounder, sharp margins
Zygomatic Arches	extends past ext. auditory meatus	extends to ext. auditory meatus
Mental Protuberance	square edge, thick protuberance	pointed edge at midline
Gonial Angles	flared <125°, wide, square	narrow >125°, constricted
Mastoid Processes	thick, thumb-like	smaller, baby finger-like
Occipital Protuberance (Nuchal Crest)	marked muscle ridges, thick	not marked, does not protrude

*Modified from Krogman, 1962:115, Brothwell, 1981:59.

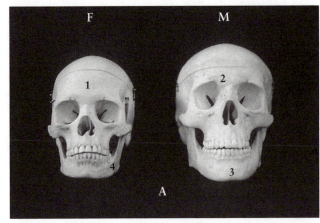

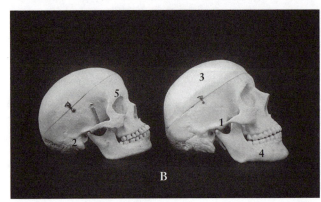

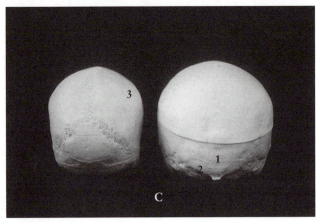

Fig. 5-6. The Female (F) and Male (M) Skull.

A. Frontal view

1. Frontal bone rounder and smooth in females, steeper and more rugged in males.

2. Supraorbital ridges are larger and more prominent in males.

3. Mental protuberance has a square edge and is thicker in males.

4. Gonial angles are narrow and constricted in females (>125°). In males they are more flared (<125°).

B. Lateral view

1. Zygomatic arches extend past the external auditory meatus in males.

2. Mastoid processes are smaller in females and are not as thick.

3. Overall, the cranium and (4) mandible are rugged and larger in males than in females within the same population.

5. The orbits have rounder and sharper superior margins in females. They are thicker and more blunt in males.

C. Occipital view

1. Occipital protuberance and (2) nuchal lines are more marked in males.

3. Parietal eminences are distinct in females, rounder in males.

The sexual dimorphic differences in the cranium, within any population, are rarely absolute but rather more intermediate. This makes it difficult to quantify the many features that differentiate males from females, especially when the traits are based on their overall shape rather than size. Though human sexual dimorphism is inherently genetic, it can also be attributed to other factors such as the environment, nutrition, diet, disease, and cultural influences, all of which affect the growth potential in males and females. Also, there may be characteristics that are based more on racial variation rather than on sex. For example, females in one population may exhibit a high, narrow pelvis, robusticity and thick brow ridges, and thus be mistaken for males from another population. With the steady increase of racially and demographically diverse populations throughout North America, along with the absence of skeletal data on these populations, the possibility of this sort of misidentification is more probable.

Age Determination

Growth Standards

A critical component of any analysis of skeletal material is age. Determining the age of an individual at the time of death provides an essential piece of information that can possibly lead to a positive identification.

Growth and development during the formative years are regular processes, and the maturation stages of various bones follow an identifiable sequence. They are therefore measurable and hence predictable under normal conditions.

Measurable traits such as dental development, tooth eruption, bone length, and the appearance and fusion of growth centers of bone, have all been collected through the years from various populations of known living and non-living individuals. Such data provide the basis of what are called *growth standards*. Growth standards are applied comparatively. The forensic anthropologist will observe the final stage of growth reached by the decedent and attempt to match this with the established standards of that particular stage. In this way, unknown skeletal material can be assigned an age with a great degree of accuracy.

Aging the Subadult vs. the Adult Skeleton

The stages of infant growth during the first six months of life are very similar in human populations. The velocity of childhood growth through to adulthood displays a regular and distinctive pattern as well. However, there are no predictable growth processes occurring in adulthood that can be measured with as great a degree of accuracy. Therefore, it is easier to assign an age to the infant or adolescent skeleton than the adult one.

Adulthood is generally marked by bone remodeling (Frost, 1985) and a steady deterioration of the skeletal system (see chapter 4). By at least the age of 25 to 30 years, changes in the subadult skeleton related to growth (lengthening and fusion) have ceased. Any bone with an articular surface or a sutural border will manifest visible changes as one ages. However, each area of the skeleton will reflect the aging process differently, depending on the bone's structure and function. For example, synovial joints undergo wear and tear, sutural borders fuse and may become obliterated, the sternal ends of ribs and parts of the articulated cartilage mineralize. These osteological changes have no consistent pattern since the rate of change depends, for the most part, on the diet, health, and physical activity of the individual.

The methods of age determination for an adult skeleton are based on the observation of wear and the deterioration of various skeletal parts. Standards for such wear and deterioration have been established over the years, derived from studies of known individuals. Todd (1920, 1921a) used dissecting room cadavers and specimens from the Western Reserve University (now known as the *Hamann-Todd Collection*); McKern and Stewart (1957) analysed the skeletons of American soldiers killed in the Korean War; and Angel et. al. (1986) examined modern forensic specimens. All of them carefully observed and recorded the subtle variations in morphology in a variety of bone in order to demonstrate the aging process.

When assigning an age to the adult skeleton, the probable disparities between *chronological age* (the actual age of the individual) and *physiological age* (the age the skeleton appears to be) are considered. Disparities between the two may be great or insignificant depending on the factors listed above. In other words, if an individual leads an unhealthy lifestyle, suffers from a chronic disease, and never exercises, his/her skeleton may look older than it actually is.

Hence, forensic anthropologists can only assign the adult skeleton a physiological age based on the state of the remains, and usually this is placed within a range: for example, an individual can be assigned an age that ranges from 30 to 45 years. This figure may or may not correspond to the individual's chronological age. The younger the individual the more narrow the age-range and conversely, the older the individual, the wider the age-range. Consequently, assigning an age to the adult skeleton will be less accurate than the one assigned to the subadult.

The following is a description of some of the more popular methods used to determine age. Whenever possible more than one method or a combination of all should be used in order to get a more accurate figure.

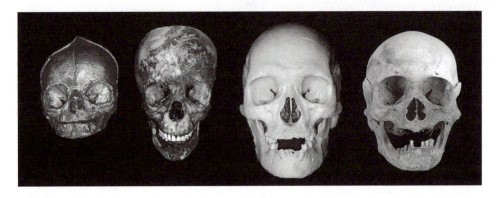

Fig. 5-7. Age progression depicted in skulls, from a fetal skull (far left) to the skull of an elderly individual (far right). Photo, Courtesy of Valeri Craigle, all rights reserved.

Age Determination and Dentition
The Non-Adult Skeleton

The growth and development of human dentition are reliable indicators of chronological age because the process is a long and continuous one, longer than that of any other organ in the body. The stages of crown formation, root development, eruption, and emergence are all identifiable and follow a particular sequence according to age and sex, and oftentimes race.

Human teeth are affected much less by environmental factors than bone is, and they are not subject to the processes of remodeling during life. Teeth are made up of very durable constituents (from roughly 96% mineral content). They are the hardest structure in the human body and last long after bone has disintegrated. As such, they provide an almost permanent source of information about an individual.

Ideally, teeth are present for analysis; however, they do not have to be anchored in the jaw (once they've erupted and matured) to arrive at an age estimate. They can be examined individually. Likewise, if teeth have not erupted above the jaw line and are still contained within the alveolar bone, as in the case of fetal, newborn, or adolescent remains, age estimates are still very accurate. Furthermore, if any form of premortem dental work was performed on an individual and there are existing dental records available for comparison, a positive

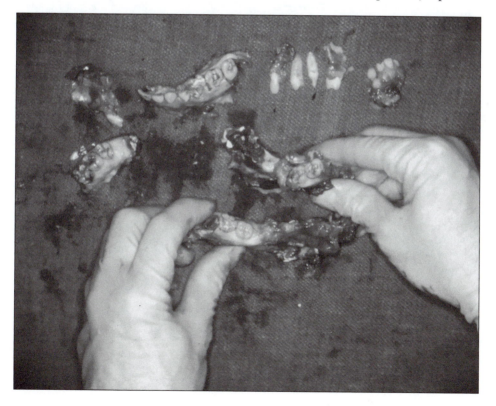

Fig. 5-8. Sorting the dental remains of an air crash victim (Photo, Courtesy of Dr. George Burgman).

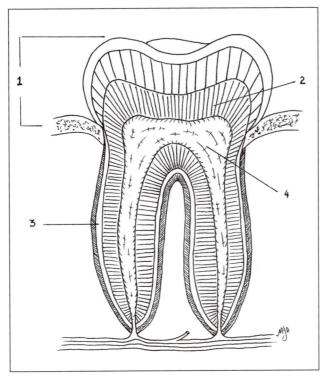

Diagram 5-1. Cross-section of Tooth.

1. Crown: composed of enamel, a calcified tissue made up of inorganic material and protein, making it the hardest tissue in the body.
2. Dentin: a bone-like substance extending from the inner surface of the enamel into the jaw to form the root.
3. Cementum: a thin layer of hard tissue covering the dentin of the root.
4. Pulp Chamber: contains a soft tissue, pulp, housing veins, arteries, and nerves, which run through the root canal.

identification is highly possible. Oftentimes, especially in the case of war and mass disasters, dental identification is all a forensic anthropologist or odontologist has to go by.

Human Dentition

Like all mammals humans have two sets of teeth: primary or *deciduous* dentition (also known as "milk teeth") and secondary or **permanent** dentition. Teeth are designed, to carry out three functions: cut, crush, and grind. The extent to which they perform each function depends on the diet. Humans are omnivorous, eating a range of meats, fish, and vegetation, and the teeth are designed to accommodate processing this variety of foods. There are incisors for holding, biting, and cutting; canines for tearing and puncturing; premolars and molars with cusps for grinding and chewing.

When teeth are developing, they do so in a top to bottom format—from the crown to the root within the alveolar bone. The development of the tooth bud in a human embryo begins in the second month after conception. Primary eruption, when the first teeth break through the gum, generally begins at six months after birth and continues through to two years of age. There are 20 deciduous teeth in total. As secondary teeth begin to develop, the roots of deciduous teeth are gradually absorbed into the bone. When a child loses a tooth, only the crown falls out when the secondary tooth dislodges it.

Secondary dentition begins to replace primary dentition around the age of 6 and continues through to 21 years of age. However, from between the ages of 6 to 13 there are combinations of both primary and secondary teeth present in various stages. After the age of 12, usually all of the primary teeth have been replaced except for the second and third molars which have not entirely erupted. The second molar erupts by the age of 13, and the third molar erupts between the ages of 17 to 21 years. The adult dentition consists of 32 permanent teeth.

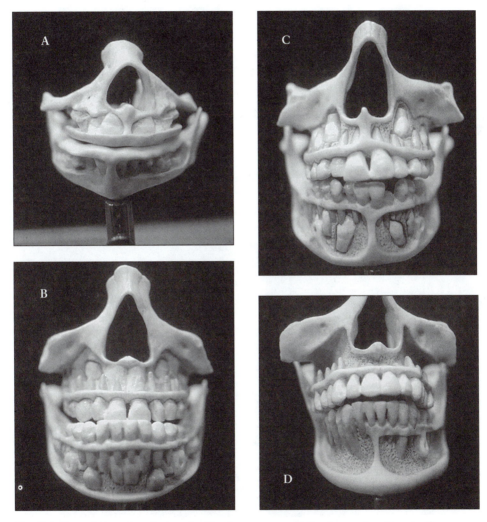

Fig. 5-9. Dental Eruption Series: A – Newborn, unerupted primary dentition in the newborn is visible in a cutaway of the maxilla and mandible; B – The dentition of a five year old. Note the primary dentition have all erupted and the growth of the secondary dentition is visible in a cutaway of the maxilla and mandible; C – In the nine year old, secondary dentition is replacing primary dentition; D – Adult dentition, secondary dentition have all erupted (Photos, Angela Milana).

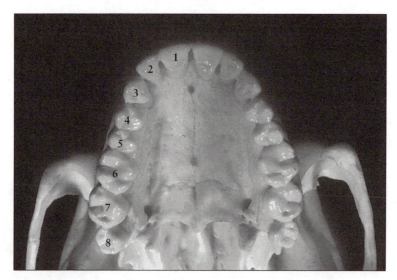

Fig. 5-10. The Maxilla (Adult Dentition).

1. Central incisor (I^1)
2. Lateral incisor (I^2)
3. Canine (C)
4. Premolar (Pm^3)

5. Premolar (Pm^4)
6. Molar (M^1)
7. Molar (M^2)
8. Molar (M^3)

Note: The letter designation represents the tooth name and the number represents the tooth position and location, i.e., superscript for maxillary and subscript for mandibular.

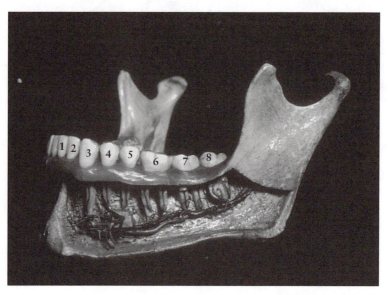

Fig. 5-11. Cutaway of the Adult Mandible. Roots of the adult dentition are visible along with the veins, arteries, and nerves.

1. Central incisor (I_1)
2. Lateral incisor (I_2)
3. Canine (C)
4. Premolar (Pm_3)

5. Premolar (Pm_4)
6. Molar (M_1)
7. Molar (M_2)
8. Molar (M_3)

Table 5-3. Average Age of Deciduous Tooth Eruption

Deciduous Teeth	Average Age of Eruption
Central Incisors	6 to 8 months
Lateral Incisors	8 to 10 months
First Molars	12 to 16 months
Canines	16 to 20 months
Second Molars	20 to 30 months

Table 5-4. Average Age of Permanent Tooth Eruption

Permanent Teeth	Average Age of Eruption
First Molars	6 to 7 years
Central Incisors	6 to 8 years
Lateral Incisors	7 to 9 years
Canines	9 to 12 years
First and Second Premolars	10 to 12 years
Second Molars	11 to 13 years
Third Molars	17 to 21 years

* Eruption times vary and upper teeth erupt later than lower teeth.

Once all of the permanent dentition has come in the stages of dental growth and development are no longer applied as an age indicator. Between the ages of 21 and 25 years, the third molars erupt and their roots develop. Beyond the age of 25, growth and developmental changes in dentition cease. The wear and deterioration in dentition begin, but the degree of both depends on an individual's diet, behavior, and health. Assessing the degree of wear and deterioration, combined with other age indicators listed below, can give an approximate age range in the adult skeleton.

Dentition and The Adult Skeleton
Cementum Annulation

A variety of methods have been developed over the last twenty years to address the problem of adult age estimation. Many of the most recent methods place an emphasis on teeth due to their durability and the fact that they undergo time-related changes that can be observed.

One of the simplest methods for dentition-based age estimation involves counting the number of teeth that remain in the dentition. As an individual ages, tooth-loss increases and there is *resorption* of the bone (loss of bone tissue). An age estimate is derived based on the absence of certain teeth and the positioning

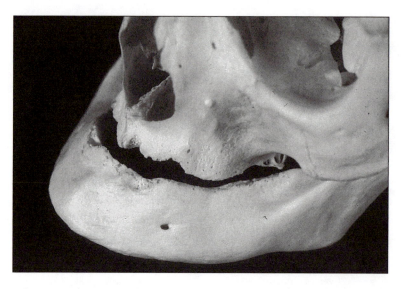

Fig. 5-12. Bone resorption in the maxilla and mandible of an elderly male (Photo, Courtesy of the V. Doucette Collection).

of those that remain (Lindemaier et al. 1989). Sometimes this method is combined with others that look at *attrition* (the wearing down of tooth surfaces), erosion, and *root resorption* (tissue loss of the root surface).

Another method of aging looks at tooth color. Teeth gradually darken with age. The organic material in teeth breakdown over time and cause yellowing and an eventual brown discoloration. According to the research, the older the individual the darker the teeth (Burchett and Christensen, 1988). To assess an individual's age based on tooth discoloration, a dental shade guide is used to compare the teeth in question (Solheim, 1988a)

The difficulty with some of the approaches listed above, however, is that they are based on conditions that are difficult to measure accurately. Though tooth loss, attrition, erosion, and discoloration are biological aging processes, they do not occur in predictable patterns in any population. They may also be dependent on factors other than age, such as culture, diet, tooth use, and health. For example, people of all ages lose their teeth for a variety of reasons: they may have them pulled for aesthetic purposes, break them in accidents, or lose them prematurely due to poor health and hygiene. Similarly, tooth discoloration, attrition, and erosion may occur due to the use of certain medications, chronic vomiting, acidic foods, and stress. Therefore, methods that assess conditions of the teeth which occur independently of these factors often yield more accurate data.

One such method looks at the growth of cementum, the hard tissue around the root of the tooth. In all mammals a thin layer of cementum is apposed around the root every year, referred to as *cementum annulation* (*rings of cementum*) (Stott et al., 1981). Why this phenomenon occurs is unknown; however, it does not seem to be related to tooth use. The consistency with which it occurs in all populations makes it a good source for age estimation in adults.

Fig. 5-13. (left) A – Sorting loose primary dentition (Photo, Angela Milana); (below) B – Scavenged human remains (Photo, John Doucette).

There are often inherent problems associated with the excavation of remains that have been intentionally dismembered, scavenged, and/or cremated. In these situations, the forensic anthropologist is often faced with the task of identifying individual broken, chipped and/or loose teeth. To assist with this process, a series of steps has been established (Anderson, 1969) to narrow the range of possibilities:

1. Determine the sort of tooth it is (deciduous or permanent).
2. Determine the type of tooth it is (canine, incisor, etc.).
3. Observe whether it is from the upper or lower jaw.
4. Distinguish on which side of the arch it originates.

Estimating age from the layers of cementum apposed over the years involves taking a very thin section of the tooth at the root and analyzing it under a light microscope. An age is obtained by adding the age at which the section of the tooth developed to the amount of rings observed, much like counting tree rings (Kvaal and Solheim, 1995).

Since the method is still quite new, there are a variety of preparation techniques being used. For example, some researchers use horizontal sections cut only through the root, while others may use longitudinal sections cut right from the crown. The optimal thickness for tooth sections has not been established. Furthermore, different developmental ages have been applied to the sections obtained. As a result, there have been some discrepancies in the correlation between the number of rings observed and known age (Rosing and Kvaal, 1998). Further research will indicate the reliability of this estimation technique for its use in forensic cases.

The Human Dentition Software Program

To teach students about the structure and function of human teeth, the Human Dentition Software Program UCSB was developed by Philip Walker et al. Computer Images of each tooth can be rotated and viewed from any angle. Along with the images are texts and diagrams illustrating diagnostic features that aid in the identification and siding of individual teeth.

Diagram 5-2. The Human
Dentition Software Pro-
gram. Courtesy of Dr. E.
Hagen, all rights reserved.

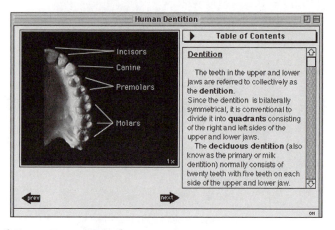

Age Determination and Long Bone Development
(Epiphyseal Union)

During prenatal development, the long bones of the skeleton are initially
formed as a cartilage model (from hyaline cartilage). In the second and third intrauterine month, this cartilaginous model begins to be replaced by bone in a
process known as *endochondral ossification*. Simply put, ossification first occurs
in the center part of the bone, the *primary center*, and from this point continues
outward until the shaft is completely ossified. The shaft part of the bone that develops from a primary center is known as the *diaphysis*.

Before puberty, *secondary centers* develop at the proximal and distal ends of
the bone, which have not yet ossified but are still separated from the shaft by a
zone of cartilage. The proximal and distal ends developing from secondary centers are referred to as *epiphyses* (singular: *epiphysis*).

The area between the diaphysis and the epiphysis remains separated by a
plate of cartilage for years in order to allow the growth in length of the bone. As
the shaft of the bone grows, it eventually unites with its proximal and distal caps,
eliminating the cartilage plate. This event is known as *epiphyseal fusion*. The
timing of this fusion, which varies according to the long bone involved, is used as
a guide in estimating the physiological age of an individual.

Assessing age based on the appearance of primary and secondary growth
centers is a relatively easier task when applied to living or very recently deceased
individuals. On excavated skeletal remains there are inherent problems involved
with this method since the age standards are based on the *degree* of fusion. Remains of children are very often incomplete due to the rapid disintegration of the
epiphyses and cartilage plates. The younger the child, the less bone there is to recover. The fragile bones that are present in fetal, neonatal, and adolescent children are usually subject to rapid erosion and are difficult to excavate. Often the
shafts become separated from their epiphyses once the cartilage plate disinte-
grates, leaving one with an incomplete skeleton to assess. To the untrained eye,
immature bone can appear non-human and can easily be overlooked.

Between the ages of approximately13 and 25 years fusion has already begun,
and bones are not as fragile. Where cartilage has disappeared there may be epiphy-

seal lines apparent, providing the basis for an approximate age. It must be emphasized, however, that there is a considerable amount of variation in the ages at which fusion begins and ends within and between populations. Furthermore, it is not an appropriate method of age determination for adults in their 30s and beyond.

Fig. 5-14. (left) The Fetal Skeleton (Photo, Angela Milana).

Fig. 5-15. (right) An immature tibia. Epiphyseal ends are separated from the shaft (Photo, John Doucette).

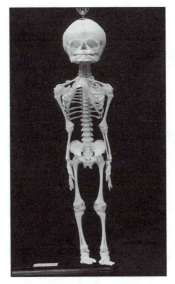

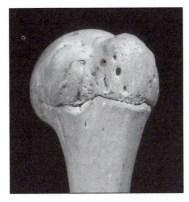

Fig. 5-16. The Humerus of a young adult. Epiphyseal line is still visible where fusion has taken place (Photo, Milana/Doucette, Courtesy of the Michener Institute of Applied Health Sciences).

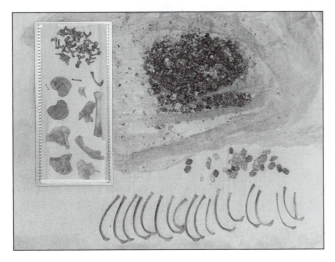

Fig. 5-17. Fetal Remains. Reprinted with permission, the Office of the Chief Coroner, Ontario.

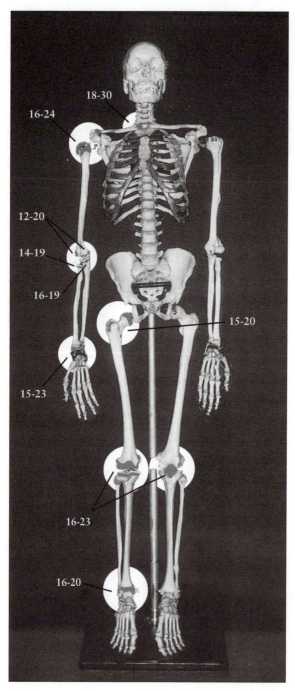

Fig. 5-18. Epiphyseal Fusion.
Highlighted parts of the skeleton
are labelled to indicate the time
span (approximate ages in years)
during which epiphyseal fusion
takes place in long bones, the
clavicle, and the patella. Ranges
differ slightly for males and
females.

Age Determination Using Sutural Closing

Unlike the long bones, the flat bones of the skull are formed from a membrane that is eventually mineralized. This process, which also involves the clavicle, the scapula, and the ribs, is referred to as *intramembranous ossification*.

There are a total of 29 bones that form the skull, each of which develops from its own center, or centers, of ossification. As the individual grows and the bones increase in size, they gradually fuse together. The sutures, located between each bone, are the areas where fusion takes place. Initial fusion begins during the first few weeks of postnatal life and continues through to the age of 21 to 35 years. In later years cranial bones fuse to the point where the sutures become obliterated. Suture obliteration can continue well past the age of 65 years and older.

There are identifiable sutures inside (*endocranial*) and outside (*ectocranial*) the skull surface and on the surface of the palate (*palatine*). The general method of determining an approximate age involves assigning a score to areas or segments of the sutures, based on their degree of closure. Usually a scale is employed in order to judge the amount of closure. Meindl & Lovejoy (1985) used a four-phase assessment to assign scores demonstrated by the following:

0	=	suture is open,
1	=	partially closed (<50%),
2	=	mostly closed (>50%),
3	=	closed.

A composite score is then determined by adding all the scores together from the various suture landmarks. This figure is then compared with an already established mean age and age range. An individual with, for example, a composite score of 11 has a mean age of 39.4, with an age range of 24 to 60 years according to the standards. Because of this wide range in possible age, it has always been advised to use this method in conjunction with others when possible. Besides, an estimate of skeletal age falling within a certain range of years does not distinguish that individual from all other individuals within the same age range.

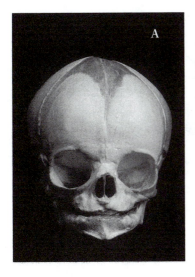
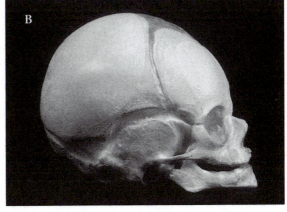

Fig. 5-19. The Fetal Skull: A–Frontal view;
B–Lateral view. Unfused bones in the fetal skull
(Photo, John Doucette).

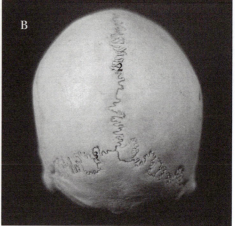

Fig. 5-20. The Adult Skull (Photo, Angela Milana).

A. Superior view of cranial sutures.   B. Occipital view of cranial sutures.

1. Coronal suture   2. Sagittal suture
2. Sagittal suture   3. Lambdoidal suture

It has been debated over the years as to whether this form of age assessment has been a useful one. According to Singer (1953), and Stewart (1979:172) the sole use of sutural closure as an age indicator is too unreliable. Loth and İşcan (1994: 406) report that sutural closure cannot be used as more than a "technique of last resort." Nevertheless, Nawrocki (1998) proposes that cranial suture closure can prove to be an effective method for age assessment when applied more thoroughly. This can be done by measuring suture closure on a larger scale (using more landmarks), using multiple areas of the vault (rather than ectocranial, endocranial or palatine sutures in isolation) and the proper application and interpretation of test samples with appropriate formulae.

Age Determination Using Pubic Symphysis Analysis

The pubic symphysis, the site where the two innominate bones articulate, is a slightly moveable joint with a disk of fibrocartilage lying between the two pubic bones. It has long been a source for age analysis due to the site's distinct morphological pattern.

Todd (1920, 1921a) first observed that the symphyseal surface of the pubis undergoes degrees of visible and textural change as one ages. He described these changes, organizing them into ten stages of development with each stage representing a five year increment. Changes he documented were those which occurred from the age of approximately 20 to age 60.

This age determination method is descriptive and based largely on comparison. In attempting to assign an approximate age to an unknown individual, one observes photographs, casts, or drawings of the successive age-related changes of the symphyseal surface and compares them to the unidentified material. Changes in the symphyseal surface relate to their shape and texture. For example, when an individual is in his/her twenties, the bony surface of the pubic symphysis is noticeably ridged and "billowy," while in the thirties, the surface is more grooved and the furrows begin to fill in. As the individual ages, the surface area becomes smoother and more concave, and the margins begin to sharpen.

Research over the years attempted to test or modify Todd's method (McKern & Stewart, 1957; Gilbert, 1973; Gilbert & McKern, 1973, Angel et al., 1986). Using collections of skeletal material, researchers established and revised standards for males and females. Todd's work apparently reflected too small a sample and could thus not adequately deal with racial variation or the differences apparent between males and females. The general concensus of the research was that the older standards could not be successfully applied to modern cases; hence, current research has attempted to gather more data using well documented forensic cases rather than older skeletal samples. Suchey et al. (1986) examined the pubic bones of over 900 males and females autopsied in Los Angeles County between 1977 to 1979. The multi-racial sample was described as more representative of a modern population. Their ages ranged from the early teens to the late 90's, verified by either birth or death certificates.

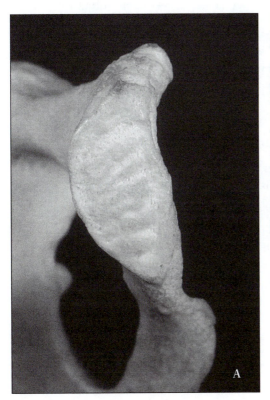
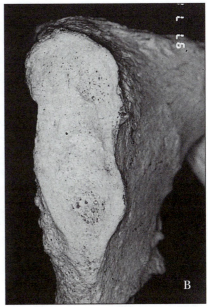

Fig. 5-21. A (top left)–Pubic symphysis of an adult female-mid 30s. Symphyseal face is noticeably ridged (Photo, Milana/ Doucette, Courtesy, The Michener Institute for Applied Health Sciences); B (top right)–Pubic symphysis of an elderly male. Symphyseal face is worn and flat with sharp margins (Photo, Courtesy of Valeri Craigle).

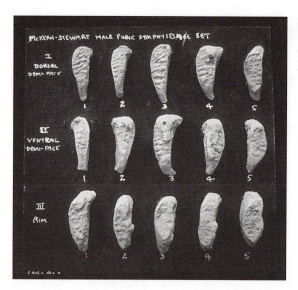

Fig. 5-22. (left) The McKern-Stewart pubic-symphysis casts, used for comparisons (Photo, Angela Milana).

Following Todd's general scheme, the original ten phases were simplified and compiled into a six-phase system referred to as the *Suchey-Brooks method* (see also: Katz and Suchey, 1986; Suchey et al., 1984). Definitions for each of the phases are modifications of those originally used by Todd. Pubic bones from forensic cases were selected and cast and made available as a kit for instructional and practical applications. Key features, the most descriptive and definitive of each phase, were highlighted in both an early and late pattern depicted as two casts for each phase. The goal was to isolate as narrow an age range as possible.

Age Determination Using Sternal Rib Analysis

The sternal end of the rib is that end which articulates with the cartilage attached to the sternum. It has been found to be a good site at which to observe age-related changes much like the pubic symphysis model described above. In 1984, physical anthropologists quantified the effects of age at this particular site using a sample study of 204 skeletons of known age, sex, and race. For the sake of consistency, they used the fourth rib from the right side (See: İşcan et al., 1984a).

The changes they observed were related to the shape of the sternal end of the rib, the size and depth of the pit within the end, and the condition of its margins. They categorized the changes that occurred over time, organizing them into a total of nine phases. The phases represent age-spans, from the mid-teen years through to the seventies. Photographs were taken of these age-related changes and put together with a description of each of the phases. Together these form two techniques referred to as *component analysis* and *phase analysis*.

Like the analysis of the pubic symphysis, the method of determining age based on the condition of the sternal rib is descriptive. The rib in question is compared with those featured in the photographs and an attempt is made to match its morphology as closely as possible.

Fig. 5-23. Sternal Rib Ends. Left to Right shows the marked deterioration of the sternal rib with aging (Photo, John Doucette).

Essentially, the sternal end of the rib in young adults appears bulbous with a surface that has been described as "billowy." The walls of the margin are thick and the bone is dense. With age, the surface begins to degrade and progressively becomes more hollowed-out, with a cup-like shape. The margins slowly become more jagged and the walls thin out. The base of the cup becomes more indented and pit-like.

According to the changes observed, it was noted that generally, females reach phases 0 to 4 at earlier ages (representing ages 13 to 32) than males, while males apparently pass through phases 5 to 8 at earlier ages (representing ages 33 to 70+) than females. Furthermore, males were described as having a "u-shaped" pit while females had more of a "v-shaped" pit (İşcan et al.,1984a; 1985). In both samples, the overall bone eventually loses density and becomes more porous with age.

The first rib standards established were based on a caucasian sample, and were sex-specific (İşcan et al., 1984a; 1985). A separate sample composed of black males and females (approximately 73 skeletons in total) showed significant differences in the patterns of age-related change and size. For example, ossification took place earlier in younger blacks (by their early twenties) making them appear older than those in the white sample (Loth and İşcan, 1987). Such conclusions were indicative of the implications of deriving standards from one population and applying them to another. Until standards are derived from samples representing a variety of populations that reflect the multi-racial make-up of North America, this method is limited in its application.

Race Determination

Social vs. Biological Concepts of Race

Groups of people are classified into "races" according to how we have learned to recognize them, that is by their geographic origins. Race classifications have also been established for historical and political reasons. The underlying notion is that racial traits reflect genetically and geographically distinct populations.

In North America, there are various notions of what makes one "Black," "White," "Asian," "Hispanic," and "Native American." These five classifications are seemingly descriptive, as they attempt to define populations that are, in reality, not genetically distinct, easily recognizable, or confined to one region. Furthermore, these limited classifications do not address racial admixture, ethnicity, or nationality.

Identifying someone racially is not as straightforward as one might think. Individuals, for example, who may be considered "White" in one country or state, may be considered "Black," "Hispanic," or both, in another. In actual fact, a racial, ethnic or nationalistic identity ultimately reflects how an individual chooses to be recognized by their family and community. This personal or community identification however may differ considerably from a societal one.

In a biological context, many of these traditional classifications have very little meaning or use. To some evolutionary biologists and physical anthropologists, the concept of race altogether is a social construct and, hence, an entirely misleading term (Evison et al., 1998; Cartmill, 1999).

Racial differences, according to the biological model, are manifested as a variety of morphological traits selected for by climatic or other ecological factors. Certain characteristics may reflect geography, others may not. Traits such as blood type, body shape, limb length, face shape, and hair form are observed as occurring in varying degrees amongst different populations, as opposed to total and distinct characteristics that genetically distinguish one population from another. Hence, individuals from different parts of the world can share many traits and have many of the same characteristics. It can also be said that for many traits, variation occurs more frequently within a population than between populations. Racial categories, in this context, are much broader and consider more ranges of characteristics.

Forensic Anthropology and Race Determination

Forensic anthropologists are usually obligated to assign a racial identity to unknown remains. Their approach, however, is less likely to reflect the biological view than the social/political one. Law enforcement personnel and the general public are often more familiar with the traditional racial categories, since a number of government agencies are involved with devising such standards (Wallman & Hodgdon, 1977). As such, forensic anthropologists must provide information that is more in line with the current legal, social, and political definitions of race.

How does this translate into assessing skeletal remains for so-called racial attributes? In short, there are no racially specific genes that manifest themselves in bone. Traits that seem to distinguish individuals from others are not unique to particular racial groups, but occur in every racial group in a wide range of variation. It ultimately comes down to identifying *degrees* of **phenotypic** traits (genetic expressions that are visible) observable in the skeleton that occur with high frequency in certain populations. Such traits include the shape of the head, nose, and face; stature; and proportions of the upper and lower limbs (Stewart, 1979;227).

Forensic anthropologists examine and measure phenotypic traits apparent on skeletal remains and compare them to those from samples of known individuals in order to determine a *likely* affiliation or ancestry. Known samples are arranged

in racial categories according to their geographic origins and the classic phenotypic traits displayed by individuals from that geographic region. Determining
race is thus based on assessing the overall similarities or differences of the unknown material to the known samples and observing the frequency and degree
with which the skeletal material displays certain traits versus others.

"The term 'race' means different things to different people"

(Stewart, 1979:227)

"Racial" Categories

Traditionally, a three-race model was used to describe broad morphological
and genetic characteristics. The races defined were Mongoloid, Caucasoid, and
Negroid, which seemingly encompassed the major race divisions. All other classifications were considered offshoots, or "sub-races" of the major three. For example, individuals of East Asian and Native American origins would be classified as
Mongoloid; while those of Mediterranean, Nordic, and East Indian origin would
be classified as Caucasoid.

More recently, a six-race model has been applied as more data on populations has become available. Gill and Rhine (1990) and Campbell (1992), among
others, describe six geographic races of the world, which is simply an expansion
of the three-race model used previously, i.e. Mongoloid, Caucasoid, Negroid,
Australoid (Melanesian/Australian), American Indian, and Polynesian. Terms
such as "Hispanic," "African-American," and "Euroamerican," describe popular
designations but are considered to be social classifications and ethnic categories.
Since they are ambiguous designations which do not conform to a biological reality, they are not considered appropriate racial classifications.

Whatever the classification scheme, however, the use of these racial categories is considered problematic primarily because it relies on the concept that
standard racial traits are inherited in a consistent pattern and can be generalized
into well-defined geographic categories (Goodman and Armelagos, 1996; Cartmill, 1999; Templeton, 1999).

Craniofacial Criteria

Assigning a race to unknown skeletal remains requires both observation and
extensive measurement. Most often skeletal traits of the face, cranium, and
mandible are first assessed. These are referred to as *craniofacial* traits. In the absence of the cranium, measurements of the postcranial skeleton are undertaken.
These however are less reliable when used alone.

Ideally, determining race should be attempted before assigning a sex due to the
variation of sexual dimorphism in different populations. Characteristics that are
common to a particular population can be confused with sex differences. For example, a large female from a more robust population could be easily mistaken for a
male from a more gracile population. Once a race, or a close approximation of

one, is assigned, then the degree of sexual dimorphism can be assessed more accurately.

For the forensic anthropologist, race determination, like other methods of assigning biological identity, requires the observation and comparison of the overall bone morphology as well as specific features on the skeleton. Assessing the skull involves looking at its basic shape and size, and the individual bones forming the facial skeleton, particularly the orbits, the nasal aperture, the maxilla, the zygomatic bones (cheekbones), and the mandible. The size and shape of the teeth are also examined as particular cultural and genetic traits may be indicative of a certain population. Lastly, the skull's profile is examined to determine whether it exhibits *prognathism*, the degree to which the upper and lower jaw projects outward. When assessed together, the presence *in varying degrees* of certain phenotypic features may indicate the possibility of the unidentified individual originating from a particular population over that of another.

Table 5-5 provides an overview of craniofacial characteristics that are used and the variations commonly attributed to each race. The four-race model is demonstrated as it is the one most often referred to in the United States. However, this is not a complete classification scheme, nor the only one used by forensic anthropologists. Furthermore, forensic anthropologists with experience recognize the limitations of this scheme, and readily acknowledge that misidentification is more than likely. The key is to understand the variations common within each population studied and to demonstrate how those variations compare with different populations. For a more in depth examination of race determination using craniofacial characteristics, the following references can be consulted: El Najjar & McWilliams, 1978; Krogman & İşcan, 1986; Steele & Bramblett, 1988; Bass, 1995; Gill, 1998.

Table 5-5. Craniofacial Characteristics in Race Determination

Characteristic	Mongoloid	Caucasoid	Negroid	Native American
Skull Height	medium	high	low	medium
Skull Breadth	broad	broad	narrow	broad
Nasal Profile	concave	straight	straight/ concave	concave
Nasal Aperture	rounded	narrow/ elongated	flared	rounded
Malars	wide/project	recede	recede/reduced	wide/project
Orbits	squared	rhomboid	rounded	rhomboid
Prognathism	moderate	reduced	extreme	moderate
Palate Shape	parabolic/ elliptic	parabolic	hyperbolic/ parabolic	elliptic/ parabolic
Mandible	robust	medium	gracile	robust
Incisors	shovel-shaped	blade-shaped	blade	shovel-shaped

Sources: Krogman, 1973; El-Najjar & McWilliams, 1978; Gill, 1998.

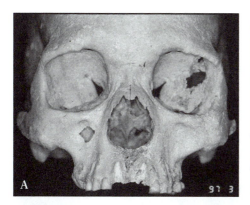 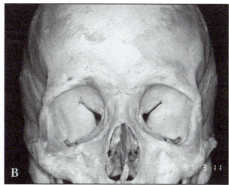

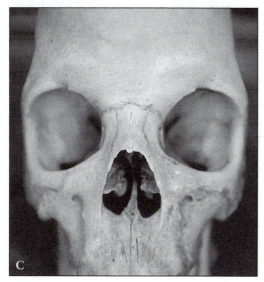

Fig. 5-24.

A (top left) – Mongoloid traits, midfacial. Malars project forward, nasal aperture is rounded, orbits are wide.

B (top right) – Caucasoid traits. Orbits are sloped, nasal aperture is narrow.

C (bottom left) – Negroid traits. Orbits are wide, nasal aperture is flared, malars recede.

(Photos, Courtesy of Valeri Craigle)

Discriminant Function Methods

In addition to the classification model outlined above, a number of metric methods are also applied by forensic anthropologists. The most widely used of these is the *discriminant function method* developed by Giles and Elliot (1962) for distinguishing American blacks, whites, and Native Americans.

The method includes taking extensive measurements of the unidentified skull, applying these figures to a set of formulae and then calculating a score. The score is then compared to a final figure termed a *sectioning point*, which is used as a basis for determining the biological affinity of the unknown. For example, if the score exceeds the sectioning point, the unknown individual may in all likelihood be black or Native American depending on the formulae used. Since the formulae varies for males and females, sex must first be determined (Giles and Elliot, 1962; Steele and Bramblett, 1988).

Estimating Stature

Regression Formulae

Formulae for estimating the living stature of an unknown individual have been developed over the years by measuring the skeleton and limb bones of known individuals. Trotter (1970), for example, examined well over 5,000 cadavers and skeletons from various collections including the Terry collection, the Smithsonian Institution, and World War II and Korean War casualties. These measurements were sorted according to population and sex, and developed as *regression formulae*. Regression formulae for stature are a set of values that are calculated along with the measurements of the unknown individual (see Table 5-5). The result is an estimate of an individual's height at death, placed within a range. Since it is only an estimate, forensic anthropologists are careful to not give exact heights, as the individual, according to the formula, could have been at least an inch shorter or taller than the calculation. Each formulae has its own range of error, and that range increases if the bones measured are damaged or fragmented.

It is necessary to know the sex and race of the individual prior to assessing his/her stature, as the formulae distinguish males from females in different racial categories. These distinctions are based on the premise that the average stature for females is less than that for males in any population and that considerable variation in stature is found among different populations (Brothwell, 1981:100).

To some extent, knowing the age of the individual is also important in that the formulae estimate maximum living stature, which is at approximately 30 years of age, the oldest age, according to Trotter, at which people reach their maximum height. Before this age individuals may still be growing, and beyond this age individuals begin to lose some height as intervertebral discs begin to degenerate and the spinal column shortens. More recent studies have suggested, however, that there is no significant loss of height until after the age of 45 years (Galloway, 1988).

If all or some of the skeletal parts are present, it is not necessary to measure each one in order to derive an estimate of stature. In fact, long bones of the leg provide a more accurate estimate of stature than other parts since they are the limbs most associated with height. However, estimates using the long bones of the arm have been derived, as have been estimates based on damaged and fragmented parts (Steele, 1970).

Using an osteometric table, the forensic anthropologist measures a long bone, typically a femur or a tibia. All measurements are taken as maximum lengths (the bone is measured end-to-end) and in centimeters. These measurements are then multiplied by the factor in the formula and added to a value. Each formula has a plus or minus error that reflects variation within a population.

Below is an example of a regression formula used to estimate the maximum living stature in American white and American black males, developed by Trotter (1970), using the maximum lengths of the femur and tibia.

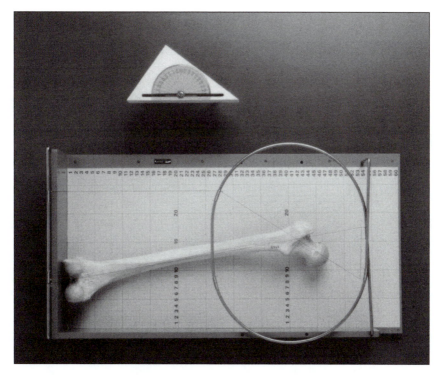

Fig. 5-25. The Osteometric Table, measures the length and angle of long bones (Photo, Courtesy of SiberHegner, Zurich).

Table 5-6. Estimating Stature

White Male

2.38 (femur) + 61.41 = Stature ± 3.27 cm

2.52 (tibia) + 78.62 = Stature ± 3.37 cm

Black Male

2.11(femur) + 70.35 = Stature ± 3.94 cm

2.19 (tibia) + 86.02 = Stature ± 3.78 cm

Note: If the length of the femur is measured at 38.1 cm, then the estimated stature according to the formula for white males would be approximately 152 cm.

As with any application of statistical formulae to living and non-living populations, regression formulae are most reliable when they are used and interpreted correctly. Errors in measurement and calculation can render inaccurate figures, as will incorrect assessments of sex, race, and age.

One must also consider the discrepancies between an individual's actual stature and that stated on antemortem records such as a driver's license, identification cards, or medical records. Various studies have shown that none of these items should be regarded as an accurate source of information regarding stature largely because stature is often self-reported and may be more a reflection of "wishful thinking" than an actual measurement (Brues, 1958). Giles and Hutchinson (1991), reviewing data from 8,000 individuals, reported that men overestimated their stature by an average of 2.5 cm, whereas women did by an average of 1 cm. Hence, the reliability of stature information reported during an individual's life must be carefully considered when compared with the estimate derived after death.

Chapter Six

Evidence of Trauma

The question of how an individual died surrounds a legal investigation when human remains are found. If investigators rely solely on the testimony of witnesses or the confessions of a perpetrator to reconstruct events, an incomplete or inaccurate account is likely. Oftentimes, interpreting the state of the remains is the only way to accurately determine what brought on an individual's demise. Thus, any evidence of trauma to a human body is suspect and becomes one of the forensic anthropologist's primary concerns because it indicates the possibility of criminal activity.

This chapter describes some of the ways forensic investigators examine human remains for signs of skeletal trauma. It also discusses their interpretation of this trauma and how it can be associated with the time of death.

Cause and Manner of Death

When investigating the death of an individual, there is an important distinction made between the *manner* and the *cause* of death. In a legal investigation there are several categories which mark the *manner* in which a person may have died; death could have been brought about by accident, suicide, homicide, natural causes, or by undetermined circumstances. The *cause* of death is the actual trauma, event, disease, or illness which starts the physiological processes resulting in death. An example of cause of death would be *asphyxia* (lack of oxygen), and whether it was self-imposed (suicide) or done by another (homicide) is an example of the manner of death.

Pathologists conducting an autopsy examine the soft tissue of the body in an attempt to determine the manner and cause of an individual's death. The standard procedure involves examining the exterior body, noting any abnormalities, and then dissecting the body in order to expose and examine the internal organs (see chapter one). There is often sufficient information in the soft tissue to establish a good picture of what took place just prior to and during the individual's death. Vital organs, by their position in the body and their size, shape and/or contents can reveal, for example, whether an individual drowned, suffocated, was asphyxiated, poisoned, shot, stabbed, strangled, or struck by a vehicle. When an autopsy concludes, if the manner and cause of death have been established, then a legal investigation will proceed should there be any evidence to suggest that the death was a homicide.

The State of the Remains

Generally, forensic anthropologists are not part of the autopsy procedure, as the remains they examine are often absent of flesh or the flesh remaining has decomposed to the point where an autopsy is not possible. The skeleton, or parts thereof, rarely offer any evidence of the actual physiological events leading to death. Individuals can sustain bone trauma without dying or die in a way that doesn't leave a mark on the skeleton. Therefore, forensic anthropologists are not often in the position to determine the manner or cause of death. Their role is to assign to remains a biological identity and to describe the state of the remains.

Bones can be recovered from a site or arrive at an anthropologist's lab in various states: intact, burned, splintered, stained, chewed, fractured, shattered, and/or fragmented. Primarily, the forensic anthropologist comments on this state and describes the likely types of objects or events which may have produced the condition in which the bones were found. Critical to all of this is the association of the state of the remains with the time of death.

When assessing the condition of the remains in order to associate this condition with the time of death, the forensic anthropologist looks for distinctive patterns, lesions, and/or identifiable marks on bone. Most of these may reflect the nature of a trauma, injury, disease or illness, but are not always indicative of the exact time at which any of the above occurred. An injury such as a fracture, for example, could have been sustained days, months or years before an individual died; during the time an individual was dying; just after death occurred; or perhaps days, months, or years after death occurred. However, there are a variety of skeletal indicators, discussed below, that can help determine the likely time that an individual sustained a particular injury or disease.

In death investigations, forensic anthropologists refer to three periods of time to distinguish when an injury took place: *antemortem* (before death), *perimortem* (around the time of or during death), and *postmortem* (after death). The point of placing the event of an injury into such periods is to understand its relevance to the case and its association, if any, with the individual's death. For example, a skull fracture that occurred years before death may not be relevant to a homicide investigation. However, if it occurred at or around the time of death, it can provide crucial evidence. In associating an injury with the time in which it was likely to have been sustained, the forensic anthropologist can sometimes help determine the manner and/or cause of death, or at least reconstruct the likely events which may have occurred during any of these three periods.

Antemortem Injuries

Whenever there is evidence of bone healing in the form of bone *remodeling,* it can be concluded that a skeletal injury was sustained before an individual's death. When the hard outer layer of bone (*cortical bone*) and the inner spongy bone (*cancellous bone*) are traumatized by a fracture, puncture, and/or break, a number of physiological events take place designed to repair the damage. Initially, the area in and around the lesion swells up and fills with blood generated

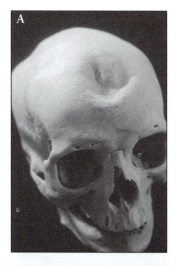

Fig. 6-1. Antemortem Trauma: A–Evidence of a healed depression fracture on frontal bone (Photo, Courtesy of The V. Doucette Collection); B–Healed fracture of the right femur (Photo, Angela Milana); C–Lateral view of a healed oblique fracture of the left humerus (Photo, Angela Milana).

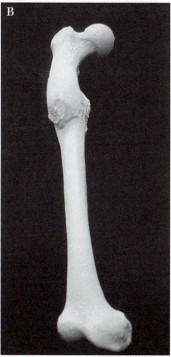

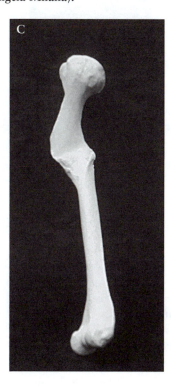

by the injured blood vessels of the bone marrow, adjacent muscles, or the **perios-teum** (the tissue covering the bone). This localized swelling is referred to as a **hematoma**. Its size depends on the nature and extent of the damage—the more serious the injury, the larger the hematoma. Plasma, the watery substance of the blood, contains proteins that eventually cause blood in the area of the lesion to clot, usually six to eight hours after the injury. Within a week, a fibrous matrix is formed within the blood clot. The fibrous matrix or **callus** forms the initial site where new bone cells are laid down to replace the ones that were damaged in the

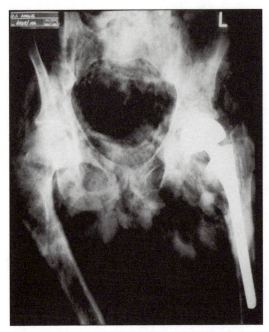

Fig. 6-2. Radiograph illustrating a hip replacement head in an elderly male. Such premortem medical records are crucial in the identification process. Reprinted with permission, the Office of the Chief Coroner, all rights reserved.

injury. The final result is remodeled bone, most of which retains a unique deformity as it is unlike the original form it has replaced.

The length of time that it takes for bone to heal and remodel depends on the nature and extent of the injury, the location of the injury, and the age and health of the individual. In young children, for instance, fractures heal quite rapidly with visible signs of remodeling (apparent in radiographs) as early as two weeks and bone consolidation within four to six weeks after the injury. In adults the process is much slower with bone taking anywhere from three to five months to consolidate (Merbs, 1989:163).

Visible evidence of healing and remodeling of injured bone usually suggests that the individual survived the injury. Bone that has healed and remodeled has a distinctive look. Healed lesions, for example, originally caused by puncture wounds or an amputation, often have rounded edges. Their surfaces are smooth, and any depression marks are filled in. Lesions caused by fractures have marked areas where the edges united. The union may be complete, indicating that the healing process was uninterrupted.

When the union between fractured bone is incomplete due to an infection or from failure to treat the injury, bone will appear more deformed, with either bone loss or significant bone growth in the area. Though it is impossible to date an actual injury simply by observing the lesion, in the event of bone remodeling it is presumed that the individual was alive when it occurred. Healing may continue up to the point of a person's death but not beyond it. Hence, if a skeletal wound is apparent, the more extensive the repair, the older the injury.

Antemortem injuries, in and of themselves, rarely give any clues to the manner or cause of death, but evidence of them can make identification of the individual possible. Premortem medical and/or dental records of a known individual must exist in order to compare with the postmortem x-rays taken of the unidentified remains. If the premortem injuries and/or past surgical procedures are the same in both x-rays, then it is most likely that the known individual and the unidentified remains are the same.

Perimortem Injuries

Skeletal lesions that have no evidence of healing usually suggest that an injury was sustained close to the time of, or just after an individual's death. Distinguishing between these two periods, however, is not straightforward and it can become even more ambiguous if one considers that the injury may have been sustained before the healing process could become evident on the skeleton. When unhealed skeletal lesions are apparent, their pattern and nature become the focus of an investigation. They are defined as perimortem injuries because their presence may be associated with the manner and/or cause of death.

When forensic anthropologists assess perimortem skeletal lesions, two important factors are considered; the nature and the cause of the lesion. The nature of the lesion refers to the type of injury incurred, such as a fracture, an amputation, or a puncture wound. The cause of the lesion refers to the implement or the event that may have caused the wound, such as a knife, an axe, or a stress injury. Determining the nature and cause of perimortem lesions along with the context in which the remains have been found often help a team of investigators establish whether a further investigation is required.

Injuries to fresh bone caused by bullets, blunt objects, and sharp instruments often present characteristic patterns that are identifiable by forensic investigators. Most can be identified with the naked eye while others require the use of a microscope, especially when the direction and angle of an injury are being examined. Below are a few examples of the nature and cause of perimortem lesions common to forensic investigators.

Bullet Wounds

A bullet is a relatively small object propelled at a very high velocity. The pattern of the wound it creates depends entirely on the type of bone it hits and the *ballistic* properties of the projectile; these include the temperature, volume, and pressure of the gases resulting from combustion, gravity, and air resistance, as well as the weight, shape, and caliber of the projectile (Spitz, 1993:311-412).

A gunshot wound to the skull leaves a pattern of penetration and fracture. The entrance hole is usually circular, beveled internally and sharply edged, while the exit hole is more ragged and beveled externally (Di Maio, 1993). Higher velocity projectiles cause greater and more rapid fracturing than lower velocity projectiles, and there may be both radiating fractures to the entry and exit wounds (Harkness et al., 1984). A lower velocity projectile may incur a smaller entry

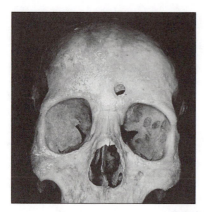

Fig. 6-3. (left) Entrance hole of a gunshot wound. Courtesy of the Utah State Office of the Medical Examiner.

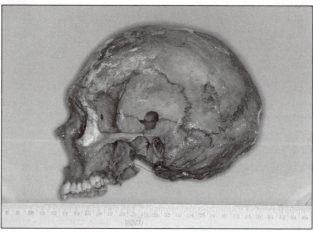

Fig. 6-4. (above) Exit hole of a gunshot wound in left temporal bone, with slight radiating fracture. Reprinted with permission, the Office of the Chief Coroner, Ontario.

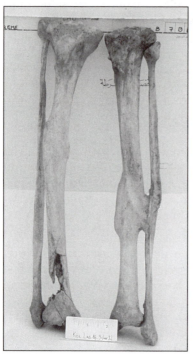

Fig. 6-5. (right) Gunshot wound to the distal end of the right tibia and fibula. Note the healed fracture involving the left tibia and fibula. Reprinted with permission, M. Doretti/EAAF Archives.

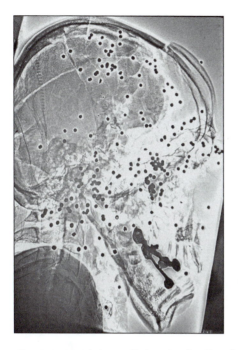

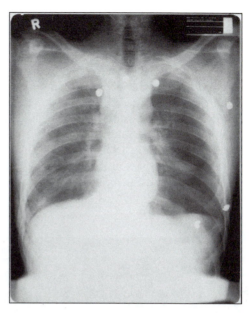

Fig. 6-6. (top left) Radiograph of pellets from gunshot dispersed within the skull. Reprinted with permission, the Office of the Chief Coroner, Ontario.

Fig. 6-7. (top right) Radiograph of bullets still lodged in chest. Reprinted with permission, the Office of the Chief Coroner, Ontario.

Fig. 6-8. (bottom right) A bullet from a 7.62 caliber firearm embedded in the sacrum. Reprinted with permission, M. Doretti /EAAF Archives.

wound with little to no fracturing, and no exit wound if the bullet remains lodged in the skull. The patterns produced by radiating fractures are important to observe, as they help in establishing the direction of the bullet as well as the entry and/or exit wounds when either or both are missing.

Gunshots to other parts of the skeleton do not leave the same pattern of fracturing as in the skull. Unless a bullet is lodged in the actual bone, there is seldom a complete bullet evident, and the marks left are often in the form of nicks and small depressions caused by the metal pellets or fragments. Bullet fragments can be dispersed throughout the body, and in decomposed or skeletal remains these will not be evident unless the remains are x-rayed.

Blunt Force Injury

A blow to the head from a blunt object such as a club can produce a de-pressed fracture. The site of impact is usually caved in, showing what is referred to as *inbending,* the size of which depends on the size of the object and the force behind it. The larger the object and the harder the blow, the wider and more caved in the depression will be. The area surrounding the site of impact will often have fracture lines that radiate away from the depression, termed *outbend-ing* (Gurdjian et al., 1950). The length and direction of the fracture lines depends on the site of impact and the force behind the blow since a fracture will take the path of least resistance and will spread until its energy is dissipated (Berryman and Symes, 1998:337).

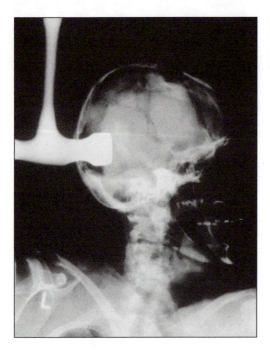

Fig. 6-9. Radiograph of a hammer still lodged in victim's skull. Reprinted with permission, the Office of the Chief Coroner, Ontario.

Fig. 6-10 Traumatic blunt force injury to medial male-olus of tibia (Photo cour-tesy of Valeri Craigle).

Sharp Force Injury

Sharp force injuries are caused by instruments such as knives, pointed implements, axes, hatchets, and the like. Each of these leaves identifying marks. The sharp edges of a knife often splinter and cut bone, creating clean or curled edges much like whittled wood. A dull edge can dent or gouge bone, leaving uneven edges. Sharp pointed instruments leave deeper and smoother holes than flat-bladed objects, which produce longer, v-shaped notches (Stewart, 1979:78).

Sometimes determining the direction of the injury and the instrument used requires the use of a scanning electron microscope. Fine details such as the marks left by the serrated edges of a knife, the nicks from a blade, or the sequence of the cut mark are not visible to the naked eye. Microscopic analysis of these can often lead to the identification of the instrument and sometimes the intent of the perpetrator.

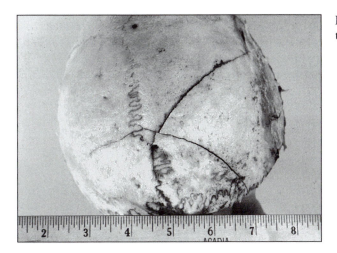

Fig. 6-11. Radiating fracture in skull, posterior view.

Fig. 6-12. Weapon is matched to site of trauma.

Fig. 6-13. Knife marks visible on sternum. Reprinted with permission, the Office of the Chief Coroner, Ontario.

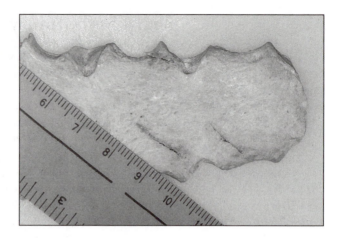

Postmortem Injuries

Any injuries and/or modifications to the skeleton occurring after an individual has died are considered to be postmortem. However, if injuries have been sustained at the time of and just after death, distinguishing between the two periods is next to impossible. Hence, these sorts of injuries are considered perimortem, even though the individual may have been dead at the time they were sustained.

Postmortem injuries or modifications are often defined as intentional versus unintentional. Intentional postmortem injuries refer to the intent and acts of a perpetrator when dealing with the remains. An example of this would be dismemberment. Unintentional postmortem injuries refers to a variety of factors that may modify or damage remains, such as animal scavenging, weather conditions, and/or poor recovery methods.

Intentional Dismemberment

Remains that have been intentionally dismembered often represent an attempt on the part of the perpetrator to hide the remains, make their identification impossible, or make their transport more manageable. Since it is necessary to cut through bone in order to take apart the human body, identifying marks are often found as remnants of this act. Knives, saws, axes, and hatchets all leave characteristic patterns, but to differentiate these patterns the marks must be viewed with a microscope. Therefore, body parts that are recovered by investigators are defleshed for a thorough skeletal analysis.

Microscopic analysis reveals that both serrated and straight-edged knife blades cutting against bone leave narrow marks with v-shaped and smooth striations. If applied to fresh bone, which is more elastic than dried, the wound closes upon withdrawal of the knife. This leaves a cut mark with less of a width than the blade that caused it (Reichs, 1998:358).

The marks left by saw blades tend to be more square in cross-section and wider than the blade itself. The striations are more visible and can be seen without a microscope since the saw blade is composed of rows of teeth with an ex-

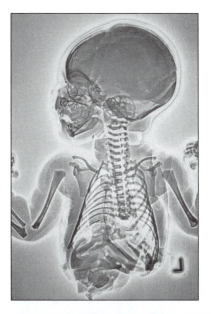

Fig. 6-14. Intentional dismemberment of infant evident on a radiograph.

Fig. 6-15. Intentional dismemberment. Close-up of saw marks on bone. Reprinted with permission, the Office of the Chief Coroner, Ontario

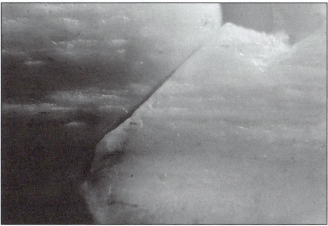

tensive cutting edge. Axes and hatchets require extensive, repetitive force and chopping action to cut through bone. As a result there may be a lot of chipping, splintering, and/or fracturing of bone, also termed *wastage* (Reichs, 1998:359). Upon inspection, cut marks are smooth and v-shaped like a knife's but much wider. Under a microscope striations are visible.

Unintentional Dismemberment

When a body is left exposed, it inevitably attracts a variety of scavengers. Though insects are usually the first to arrive, they feed exclusively on flesh, burrowing into orifices and open wounds. Their feeding and reproductive activity do not damage bone. Birds and small animals feed off the most accessible fleshy parts like the lips, cheeks, eyes, and ears. Carnivores including dogs, wolves, coy-

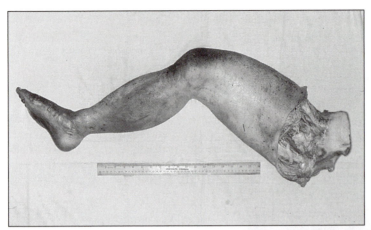

Fig. 6-16. A (above) – Traumatic dismemberment caused by the hydro-electric turbines in Niagara Falls; B (right) – Defleshed bone from the same leg reveals the rough edges indicative of such dismemberment.

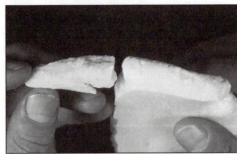

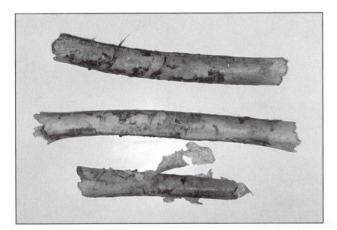

Fig. 6-17. (above) Canid scavenging. Note chew marks and ragged edges of the bone.

Fig. 6-18. (right) The uneven striations of rodent gnaw marks on bone. Reprinted with permission, the Office of the Chief Coroner, Ontario.

otes, and bears will eat the available soft tissue as well as chew or gnaw on the remaining bones. The noncarnivores such as rodents, raccoons, and porcupines often arrive to gnaw on defleshed bone, deriving minerals from it and keeping their teeth sharp.

Dismemberment that occurs due to animal activity has a very different look and pattern. Bones that have been chewed bear impressions of teeth; the edges are generally more ragged with deep grooves, scratches, and fragmentation. The ends of long bones are often chewed first as these are areas rich in marrow. Without these distinctive articular surfaces, the remaining shafts that are fragmented are difficult to identify and can be confused with other species. This is especially the case when they are dragged away into animal lairs or dens where they may be commingled with other animal bones.

If the individual was killed by an animal, then any damage to the skeleton is considered perimortem. Most cases of animal scavenging are postmortem, but an individual's body does not have to be outdoors for this to occur. For example, there have been many reported cases of animal scavenging by domestic house pets after a pet owner has died. Dogs and cats have been known to eat their deceased owners when confined with their bodies and no other food source.

Damage to the skeleton that occurs long after the individual's death is often recognizable due to the differences between fresh and old bone. Fresh bone is softer, more elastic and moist. This makes it more pliable, so when it is fractured it splinters and has more irregular edges that remain attached. Old bone is dry and brittle and therefore shatters more readily, with cleaner edges and regular fragments. New surfaces that are exposed in old bone as a result of breaking or cracking will often be lighter in color indicating that the break was postmortem.

Burned Bone

The bodies of individuals who have been trapped in burning structures, in vehicles, have set themselves on fire, or were intentionally burned to dispose of their remains can still be identified in many instances. In fires that are of short duration, like those occurring in small structures and vehicles, a good portion of the skeleton can survive the firing process, and the burned skeletal remains will still be good indicators for age, sex, and race. In cases where the skeleton has been reduced to very small fragments and ash, as in the case of cremation, identification is next to impossible unless fragments of the skeleton are recognizable. In both scenarios, identification is made more possible with antemortem dental and medical records that can be compared with the remains and/or items that have survived with the remains, such as dental appliances, surgical implements, and orthopedic devices.

Though the skeleton is not destroyed in short duration fires, it is considerably reduced in size to many bits and pieces. Prolonged firing of bone that contains flesh causes the intact bone marrow to heat and quickly expand, eventually causing it to shatter. Within a skull, the dense tissue and the brain matter expand, creating enough internal pressure to cause the skull to explode, pieces of which may be scattered some distance from their original site. Limb bones are re-

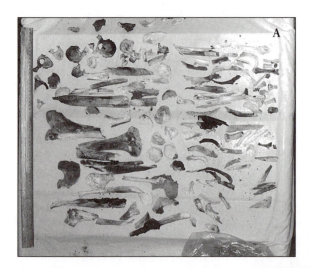

Fig. 6-19. A–An assemblage
of burned bone; B–The deep
fracture lines of fleshed bone
that has been burned; C–The
remains from a short duration
fire. Blackened remnants of skin
and clothing are still evident.
Reprinted with permission, the
Office of the Chief Coroner,
Ontario.

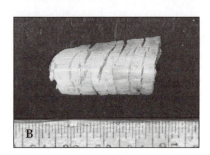

duced to less than half their original length, and ribs usually burn down to small
stubs protruding from the vertebral column. The longer the fire and the more in-
tense the heat, the more reduced the skeleton will be (Maples, 1995).

Fleshed bone ("green bone") burns differently from dry bone due to the difference in moisture and fat content. When bone with flesh attached is burned,
deep transverse fracture lines appear on the bone because of the expansion and
pressure caused by the heating of intact flesh. There is also considerable warping,
and blackened tissue on or within the bone may still be apparent. Conversely,
dry bone that has been burned has very little warping with longitudinal fracture
lines, and some superficial cracking (Binford, 1972:376).

The task of sorting through all of the bits and pieces of burned bone is a long
and arduous one. Primarily, pieces are often sorted and organized by size and
shape. Flat bones and irregular shaped bones are placed together as they are normally associated with bones from the axial skeleton, i.e. the skull, scapula, sternum, ribs, vertebral column, and pelvis. Whereas bones with a remaining shaft
and a small or large diameter represent the appendicular skeleton, the upper and
lower limbs. Ideally, some of the pieces can be fitted and glued together to the
point where they can be measured and examined more completely.

Table 6-1. Trauma To Bone-Characteristic Patterns

Source of Trauma	Size/Type of Implement	Area of Trauma	Characteristic Pattern
Bullet	high velocity	skull	– rapid fracturing
			– radiating fractures to entry and exit wounds
			– entrance hole circular, beveled internally with sharp edges
			– exit hole ragged and beveled externally
	low velocity	skull	– incurs a smaller entry wound with little to no fracturing
			– no exit wound as bullet may be lodged in skull
Blunt Object	club, head of hammer, mallet	skull	– produces depressed fracture (in-bending), the size of which depends on the object and force of blow
			– fracture lines radiate away from depression (outbending)
Sharp Implement	knife (serrated & straight-edged)	bone	– leaves narrow marks – splinters bone, creating clean or curled edges
			– dull edge can dent/gouge bone, with uneven edges
			– v-shaped and smooth striations (in cases of dismemberment)
			– cut mark less in width than blade size (in fresh bone)
	saw blade	bone	– marks are square and wide in cross-section
			– striations visible
	axe/hatchet	bone	– produces chipping, splintering, fracturing of bone (wastage)
			– cut marks are smooth, v-shaped and wide
			– striations visible
Animal Scavenging	chewing, biting gnawing	bone	– bone bears impression of teeth – edges are ragged with deep grooves
			– bone may be splintered, fragmented
			– gnaw marks of rodents visible as uneven striations

Chapter Seven

Reconstructing Identity

Chapter seven looks at some of the advances in forensic science, primarily in the fields of facial reconstruction and DNA analysis; two areas that are often intimately involved with reconstructing the identities of both victim and perpetrator. Although these investigative methods have been controversial in the past they continue to draw from an array of scientific research, advances in imaging techniques, and computer technology. Technically, facial reconstruction methods and DNA analysis are not extensions of forensic anthropology; however, many forensic anthropologists have incorporated, as well as contributed to, the methods and techniques used in both fields.

Advances in many areas of forensic science reflect the interaction between technology and problem solving. Legal investigations almost wholly rely on newer and faster ways to isolate physical evidence to keep them ahead of increasingly sophisticated crimes. Since forensic science is an eclectic field that continually borrows from other disciplines, there are an abundance of methods and techniques to draw from, making this one of the fastest growing areas of science to date. For further reading on this topic see: Kaye, 1995; Eckert, 1997; Freeman and Reece, 1998; Nickell and Fischer, 1999.

Facial Reconstruction

Facial reconstruction is a complex process that combines knowledge of human anatomy with artistic ability. A variety of methods have evolved over the years, demonstrating a progression from the purely artistic approach, with the emphasis on technique and skill, to the more scientific approach using revised data and sophisticated technology.

Beginning in the 19th century scientists, primarily in Germany, gathered information on the shape and size of the skull together with the depths of the soft tissue of the face. By sticking things like knife blades (Welcker, 1883), pins (Kollman, 1898), and sewing needles (His, 1895) into cadavers, measurements of the flesh around the scalp, eyes, cheeks, forehead, and chin were recorded and standardized. These measurements formed the basis for the "plastic" three-dimensional method of facial reconstruction and the two-dimensional facial drawing.

The Plastic Three-Dimensional Method

The plastic three-dimensional method uses clay, wax, or plasticine to rebuild the face directly over the skull (or a cast of the skull). Tissue-depth markers, in the form of pegs, are glued along the landmarks of the skull to demarcate areas where the flesh thickness varies. The clay, wax or plasticine is used to fill the spaces in between the pegs in the way of muscle and skin. These are built up in layers much like facial muscles and tissue. Artificial eyes are placed into the orbits, and accessories such as wigs, facial hair, glasses, or jewelry may be added to enhance the final reconstruction (see Fig.7.1)

This method first became popular at the turn of the last century where it was applied predominately to archaeological finds and famous historic cases, as in the facial reconstructions of Bach (His, 1895), Kant (Welcker, 1883), Raphael (Welcker, 1884), and Dante (Kollman, 1898).

The process of three-dimensional facial reconstruction during the late 19th and early 20th century, however, was highly subjective. Methods were based largely on the artist's ability to recreate a famous face. Historic grave sites often contained more than one body, were poorly marked, and were often looted. Prior to reburying the remains of a famous individual, the skull in question needed to be authenticated. In archaeological casework during the same period, facial reconstructions were applied to casts of early hominid fossils. These were placed in museum displays to fascinate the public, and bring them "face to face" with the past.

Three-dimensional facial reconstruction for forensic purposes was first introduced in Britain in the late 1920s. In North America it did not catch on until the 1940s (Krogman, 1946). Unlike its archaeological counterpart, the goal of forensic facial reconstruction was to produce as close a likeness as possible of the once living individual. But from the 1920s through to the 1960s facial reconstruction for forensic use was unpopular. Studies such as the one conducted by a scientist named Von Eggeling in the early 1900s (Gerasimov, 1968) implied that the process rendered inaccurate results, and was too subjective for use as an investigative method. He sent skull casts of a deceased individual to two different artists for reconstruction and in turn received two different faces.

In the late 1960s facial reconstruction for use in forensic cases experienced a revival. Anthropologists in the United States, Russia, and Britain began to test the validity of the plastic method as more and more reconstructions were successfully identified. Snow et al. (1970) for example, working for the Federal Aviation Authority's Aeromedical Institute mounted photographs of completed facial reproductions of a male and a female above a series of antemortem photographs of different individuals including the deceased. He then distributed them to police officers and civilians to see whether they could match the facial reproduction with the correct photograph. The male was identified correctly by two-thirds of the group of individuals who viewed the photographs, while the female was identified correctly by only a quarter of the group. The antemortem photograph of the female was taken 25 years before her death, so the results in this case were stated as being above the expected range.

Though the three-dimensional method still employed the same measurements obtained from a small sample of cadavers from the last century, the technique of forensic facial reconstruction was gaining acceptance as a viable method of identification. Despite continued questions surrounding its accuracy, it was an exciting method that seemed to draw tremendous support from the public.

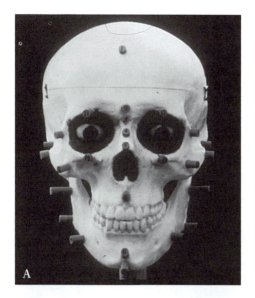

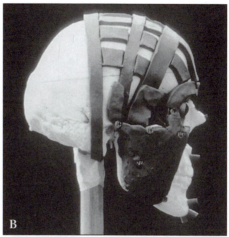

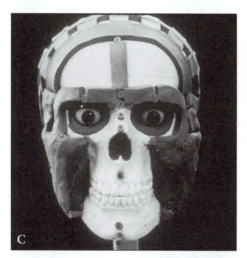

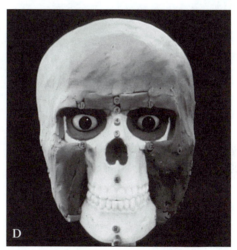

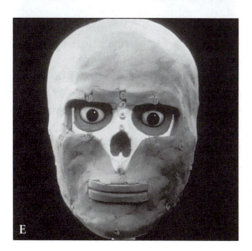

Fig. 7-1. The process of three-dimensional facial reconstruction. Reconstruction, Barbara Burgman, photos courtesy of Dr. George Burgman, all rights reserved.

A – Artificial eyes in the orbits stare at the viewer. Tissue-thickness pegs are in place.

B to E – A plasticine framework is wrapped onto the skull and the intervening spaces are filled in to form the muscle and flesh.

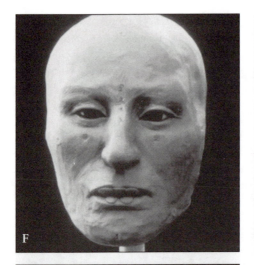

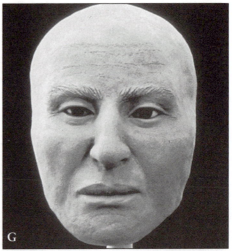

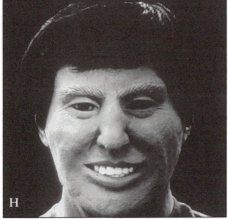

Fig. 7-1. (cont.)

F to G–Finishing touches to the lips, eye-lids and brows.

H–A wig and a smile complete the recon-struction.

Revising Old Standards

Since the turn of the last century, scientists questioned the use of facial mea-surements drawn from cadavers. Their primary argument was based on their ob-servation of the rapid changes in the human body after death, most notably the loss of fluids from the face. It was noted that soft tissue depths taken from this area were inaccurate and, when applied to unidentified skulls, would result in faces that were "less fleshier" than their once living subjects (Evison et al., 1997). The sample of cadavers originally used was small, lacking variation in age, sex, and race. Therefore, the measurement standards established could not accurately reflect the variety of size and shape differences apparent in males and females within a multi-racial, multi-age population.

By the mid-1980s new soft-tissue data became available, as well as new techniques in taking these measurements. Rather than sticking pins and nee-dles into cadavers to measure the thickness of their facial tissue, techniques using ultrasound and images of craniographs enabled scientists to obtain data from samples of living individuals (Hodson et al., 1985; Dumont, 1986;

George, 1987). However, the sample sizes were admittedly small and were still not varied enough, in terms of age and race, to merit substantial changes in the field.

The advances over the past years in research and data for this method of facial reconstruction have been minimal. It is still considered to be a highly subjective approach for identifying missing or deceased individuals. This is partly due to the fact that unique traits such as eyelid shape, lip fullness, hairlines, and skinfold patterns that are not apparent on the skull have always been guesswork. Whether or not these traits actually affect the chances of a person being recognized is a key question. Pragg and Neave (1997) state that since there are too many variables, a three-dimensional reconstruction based only on the skull cannot be completely accurate, and should never be regarded as a portrait.

Forensic anthropologists are careful to refer to the reconstructions as facial "approximations" rather than actual reproductions. They are designed to trigger recognition in the viewer, creating the possibility of a positive identification. However, the current success rates for identification resulting from facial reconstruction are roughly 50% (Archer, 1998).

The process of making a cast from a skull, placing soft-tissue depth markers in place, and rebuilding the soft tissue from clay or plasticine is time consuming and labor intensive. Making adjustments to the finished reconstructions or altering features once they are completed is difficult. As such, the three-dimensional facial reconstructions are usually employed when other methods of identification are impossible or have failed to produce results.

Two-Dimensional Facial Reconstruction

The two-dimensional method of facial reconstruction is the drawing of a facial likeness from the skull. It has always been the primary technique of identification carried out by police artists and trained forensic anthropologists.

Referred to as the "police sketch" or the "artist's composite," the traditional two- dimensional reconstruction method often used kits containing features such as eye, cheekbone and jaw shape collected over the years by forensic personnel. These features were assembled together by hand, according to eyewitness accounts or family descriptions, to form a composite drawing.

Alternatively, the composite was created by plotting the appropriate tissue-depths onto the skull—the same as those applied to the three-dimensional method, photographing, or x-raying the skull—and then tracing specific features on paper over the actual photograph or radiograph (Cherry and Angel, 1977; Krogman and Iscan, 1986). The style and type of hair type would be determined either by samples found on the scene or by estimation determined by the victim's age, race and sex.

The use of the two-dimensional method for forensic casework in the United States has been a long and consistent one throughout the last century, though currently the manual method is not as popular due to computer advancements. These are discussed below.

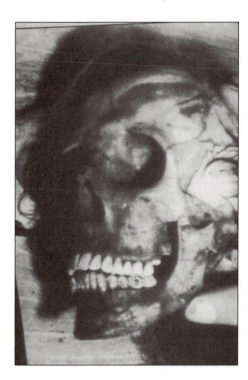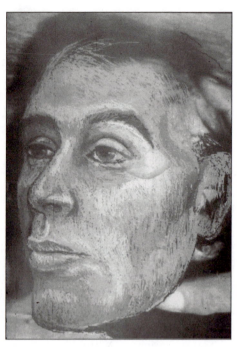

Fig. 7.2 A–B. Two-Dimensional facial reconstruction drawn from the skull of an unidentified male. Photo courtesy of Toronto Police Services, all rights reserved.

Computerized Methods

The advent of computerized methods has ushered in a whole new era in facial reconstruction. Most of the methods developed over the last 10 years utilize
computer software to aid the plastic three-dimensional reconstruction. Tissue-
thickness data are based on revised cadaver samples, or more recently, from living individuals using ultrasound techniques (Lebedinskaya et al., 1993). Facial
tissue-depths in the form of pegs are glued onto the skull at their appropriate
landmarks. An image of the skull with the pegs in place is then scanned onto the
computer, which can then be stored and used as a template. Clay or plasticine is
then applied to the skull and the features are sculpted. The computer enhances
these features further so the sculpting does not have to be as detailed. With the
use of a video camera or another digitizing device, the image of the sculpted skull
is then processed digitally (Vanezis et al., 1989; Ubelaker and O'Donnell, 1992;
Shahrom et al., 1996).

The use of the computer, in this case, does not make the facial reproductions
more accurate or exact. It enhances the three-dimensional reconstruction by providing multiple variations of the same image and enabling fast alterations to features. For example, hair color and style; the shape of the eyes, ears, or nose; the
hairline and any facial hair can be continually adjusted depending on the evidence obtained. Also, accessories such as jewelry, eyeglasses, and items of clothing that may have been recovered along with the skeletal remains could be incorporated into the image.

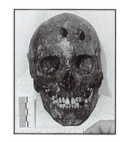

Fig. 7-3. A (above)–CARES reconstruction from skull of female next to actual photo, after identification was made; B (below)–CARES reconstruction from skull of unidentified female.

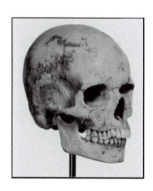
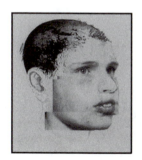
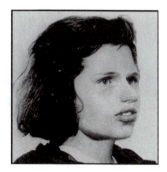

Fig. 7-4. Image of missing female aligned to image of a found cranium, match is positive. Photos courtesy of Betty Clark, Toronto Police Services, all rights reserved.

Software programs, such as CARES (Computer Assisted Reconstruction and Enhancement System), FACE, and another called "Faces," use radiographs or photographs of faces or skulls. These are then digitized, and using banks of stored facial features, a face is electronically restored or reconstructed (Ubelaker and O'Donnell, 1992).

The computer has enabled the reconstruction process to be a fast, reproducible and increasingly more precise method. In addition to this, medical imaging techniques are currently used in place of measurements derived from cadaver samples. Data can now be imported directly from images produced by hospital procedures, such as the computed tomography (CT) scan (see Fig 7-7) and magnetic resonance imaging (MRI). These high- resolution images from a variety of living individuals provide numerous and accurate measurements of facial tissue depths.

Nonetheless, practitioners in the field find that there are still inherent difficulties associated with facial reconstruction. Reichs and Craigs (1998: 507) state that there is still a shortage of up-to-date tissue depth information for different ages and populations combined with a lack of standardization for approximating facial features such as eyes, ears, nose, and lips. To date, there is also no way of predicting individual characteristics not apparent on the skull, such as hairstyle, facial hair, dimples and superficial scars. Thus, the two and three-dimensional facial reconstruction, with or without the aid of a computer, cannot be considered the primary means of positive identification. They are methods which still serve to excite public curiosity however, as stated earlier, they are often used as a last resort when other identification methods have failed.

Fig. 7-5. Scanning the skull for computer imaging. Image courtesy of the Department of Forensic Pathology, University of Sheffield.

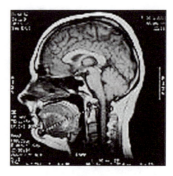

Fig. 7-6. The use of a CT scan for deriving more accurate data on tissue thickness. Image courtesy of the Department of Forensic Pathology, University of Sheffield.

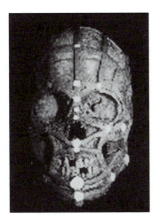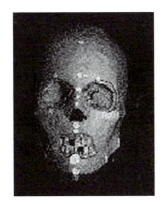

Fig. 7-7. Computerized facial reconstruction. Images courtesy of the Department of Forensic Pathology, University of Sheffield.

DNA Analysis

Over the past ten years, research on molecular genetics has seen a dramatic rise, accompanied with highly innovative computer technology and sophisticated imaging techniques. Assessing an individual's genetic profile, as in the DNA "fingerprint," has become a worldwide method of analysis used in rape and homicide investigations as well as in cases of assessing ancient remains. This highly complex method has been portrayed as an effective means of understanding biological relationships and examining the genetic bases of disease across vast amounts of time and space.

Much like the use of actual fingerprint analysis at the turn of the last century, DNA fingerprinting has had a major impact on the way criminals are pursued and convicted. In the hands of forensic scientists, minute samples of bodily fluids, hair, skin, and bone can be processed to reveal a genetic identity in the form of a mysterious collection of bands on a computer screen. The power of such evidence has already led to the conviction of thousands at the same time that it has enabled hundreds of others to be released from life imprisonment or death sentences.

Generally forensic anthropologists do not process DNA as part of their skeletal analysis. It is a method of identification carried out primarily by forensic biologists. DNA can be extracted from bone, and sex can be determined from an unidentified sample. This is undoubtedly a faster and more accurate method than a morphological assessment of the skull and pelvis. However, it is standard protocol in legal investigations to primarily assess the DNA of presumed perpetrators, a task not undertaken by forensic anthropologists. The act of processing the DNA of an unidentified individual for personal identification may be a method applied in the future, but currently it is not undertaken for legal reasons (see below). DNA analysis does not render forensic anthropology obsolete but in fact complements it.

The following section discusses the fundamentals of this highly charged area of analysis, beginning with a brief description of what DNA is and the methods used by forensic scientists to create the so-called "fingerprint."

DNA-Structure and Function

Deoxyribonucleic acid (DNA) is the fundamental "blueprint" of all living matter, the genetic information that dictates the form and development of an organism. Structurally, it is a two-stranded molecule composed of chemical compounds. Containing an enormous amount of information, the strands of a DNA molecule are arranged as a *double helix*, a twisted, staircase-like structure, and efficiently packed into the nucleus of each cell.

Each strand of the helix consists of long chains of *nucleotides*. *Nucleotides* are each composed of a phosphate group, a type of sugar called deoxyribose, and one of four nitrogen containing bases. The bases are *adenine* (abbreviated as **A**), *thymine* (**T**), *guanine* (**G**), and *cytosine* (**C**). Hydrogen bonds between the bases of each strand hold the double helix together in a regular and specific pattern: i.e. adenine (A) will only bond with nucleotides containing thymine (T), and guanine (G) will only bond with nucleotides containing cytosine (C). These subunits form what are called *base pairs* (**bp**).

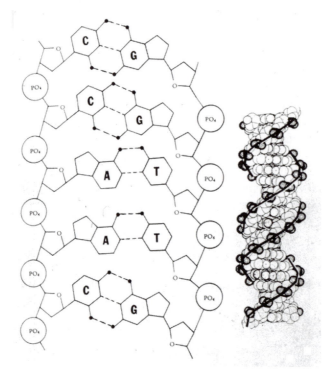

Diagram 7-1. The DNA Double Helix (right).

Unfolded (left), the nucleotides are evident, each composed of a phosphate group, deoxyribose and one of four nitrogen containing bases, adenine (A), thymine (T), guanine (G) and cytosine (C). The hydrogen bonds between the bases of each strand hold the double helix together in a regular and specific pattern, A-T and G-C, making up what are known as base pairs.

Strands of DNA make up codes for particular proteins, referred to as **genes**, that provide genetic information in the organism, for example, eye color, height, hair texture and skin color. Most human genes appear to be made up of 5 to 10,000 base pairs (AT or CG pairs) but some may be made up of several hundred thousand. However, not all human genes have been identified at this time, that is, the sequences of their base pairs have not yet been determined.

DNA strands also contain non-coding sections that apparently provide no relevant genetic material, or what they code is unknown at this time. These parts of the strands were long referred to as "junk DNA" because scientists didn't understand their function. However, current research in the field has proven that various segments of non-coding DNA are vitally important for the proper regulation and translation of genes (McElwee, 1998). In humans, at least 10 % of our DNA represents actual genetic information while approximately 90% of our DNA is made up of this non-coding "junk" (Krawczak and Schmidtke, 1998:11-13).

As a long, continuous series of base pair sequences a DNA molecule would extend 9400 miles in length (at ten base pairs per inch) if it were stretched out (DNA is measured in **angstroms** which is a hundred-millionths of a centimeter). The "packages" carrying these molecular strands are known as **chromosomes**. There is one molecule of DNA in each chromosome (chromosomes range in size from 50 million to 250 million bases) and every species has a characteristic set of chromosomes. One cell's collection of chromosomes is known as a **genome**. Humans inherit a genome of 23 chromosomes from each parent.

Though the chemical structure of DNA is the same for all cellular organisms, it is the length and sequence of the base pairs along the DNA strands that differ within and between species. For example, the base pair sequences that code for traits such as 10 fingers and 10 toes are identical in all primates including humans, but the base pair sequences that code for the size, shape, and color of those ten fingers and toes are unique in each individual. Alternatively, one can think of DNA as a type of genetic phone number. Each species has an area code, but each individual has their own telephone number made up of millions of digits rather than the standard seven!

The length of DNA is measured by the amount of base pairs (bp) in its strand and this varies greatly depending on the organism. One thousand base pairs are abbreviated as **kb**, and **Mb** represents one million base pairs. One should imagine that the more complex the organism, the more base pairs to their DNA, but consider the fact that the genome of a butterfly (*Fritillaria assyriaca*) is 124,900 Mb, while the human genome is a mere 3,000 Mb! Why a butterfly would need more DNA than a human is a question that remains unanswered.

Case # 1: DNA "Fingerprinting"

In 1986 in the small English village of Narborough, police were in the midst of investigating the rape and murder of two 15-year-old girls. The murders had been committed three years apart but based on the patterns displayed at both crime scenes, police suspected they were committed by the same individual.

Shortly after the second murder in 1986, a tip-off led the police to arrest a 17- year-old employee at the local mental institution. He confessed to one of the murders but denied any involvement with the other.

During this period of time, a genetics professor, Dr. Alec Jeffreys of Leicester University, England, had been studying DNA variation and the evolution of gene families. He was interested in trying to detect inherited variation within genes between different individuals. Dr. Jeffreys' aim was to develop *markers* (a type of identification tag) to track the position of these genes.

In 1980, Dr. Jeffreys' lab had produced one of the first descriptions of what are termed *Restriction Fragment Length Polymorphisms* (RFLPs). RFLPs are DNA *restriction fragments* (sections of DNA on a particular chromosome that have been cut into fragments by an enzyme), that vary in length between individuals within the same species. The cause of the length difference was found to be the result of a variation in base pair sequences. It was also found that some of these sequences repeated themselves in particular patterns inherited from one or both parents. Subsequently, Jeffreys and his colleagues described a general method for accessing large numbers of these highly variable regions of human DNA from bodily substances, and processing them for observation and comparison (Jeffreys, 1985a).

By 1984, Dr. Jeffreys successfully tested the use of DNA analysis for identification purposes. When the DNA of several individuals was processed (see below for the methods used) different banding patterns were seen for different individuals. The image produced by this banding pattern of DNA was dubbed a "fingerprint" because of its ability to differentiate between individuals (Jeffreys et al., 1985b).

This breakthrough in genetic identification led police in Narborough to send Dr. Jeffreys samples of the semen found on both victims along with a blood sample from the 17-year-old individual who had confessed. The DNA banding patterns showed that the semen samples were indeed from the same individual; however, they did not match the DNA extracted from the blood sample. Realizing that the confession from the 17-year-old had been a false one, police released the suspect from custody, marking this event as the first case where DNA analysis had eliminated a suspect.

Based on the semen samples analysed, police were armed with the true assailant's genetic identity. Launching the world's first genetic manhunt, police in Narborough collected blood samples from males in the vicinity between the ages of 13 and 35. Over 5,000 blood samples were submitted for forensic analysis.

Several months into the processing of the blood samples, a break in the case came when someone tipped police that they had overheard a man boasting at how he had paid someone to submit a blood sample in his place. When approached by police and confronted with the murder accusations, the individual quickly confessed convinced that his blood would "give him away" (Proctor et al., 1998).

In 1987, the 27-year-old assailant was arrested, his blood was tested and his DNA was found to match the DNA extracted from the semen samples taken from the two murdered girls. He was convicted and is currently serving two life sentences.

"Fingerprinting" vs. "Typing"

Since the pivotal Narborough case, DNA "fingerprinting" has become one of the most popular areas of forensic science. Different methods of extracting and analyzing DNA from human, animal, plant, bacterial, and viral samples have evolved throughout Europe and North America alongside major advances in genetics research and technology.

The terminology describing various DNA extraction, processing, and analytic methods has also changed, which has lead to some confusion outside of the field. Popular terms such as DNA fingerprinting, DNA typing and DNA profiling have been used interchangeably to refer to the act of processing DNA as physical evidence. Each term, however, denotes a specific process that differs quite substantially from the next.

DNA *typing* describes the system of assessing variation in sections of DNA for analysis. Hence, one can use the term "DNA typing" or "DNA typing systems" to refer to a variety of methods which isolate and extract sections of DNA (plant, animal, viral, and/or bacterial) for observation and comparison.

DNA *fingerprinting* is the original method (a first generation typing system) developed by Dr. Jeffreys and his colleagues in the mid-1980s (Jeffreys, 1985b). Simply stated, fingerprinting looks at sections of DNA located in different regions on different chromosomes, which is why it is also referred to as a "multi-locus" typing system. Fingerprinting produces patterns that are entirely unique to an individual except in identical twins. The results are usually rendered as a sequence resembling a bar-code.

DNA *profiling* is a more recent development (a second generation typing system) that looks at one area on a specific chromosome (single-locus). Profiling produces patterns that unrelated people are most unlikely to share. The probability of individuals matching varies considerably and depends entirely on the section of DNA examined. However, close relatives, especially siblings, are likely to share patterns produced by this form of DNA typing, hence the traits are not entirely unique in a population, and so they are not considered fingerprints. For further reading on this topic see: Krawczak and Schmidtke, 1998; Billings, 1992; Ballantyne et al., 1989.

Methods of DNA Typing

Most human DNA shows very little variation between individuals; in fact 99.9% of it is identical among humans (Blake, 1999). The small percentage that is different between individuals is the basis for the fingerprinting and profiling used in medical research, genetics, and forensic science.

Since DNA is found in every cell with a nucleus, it can be extracted from bodily substances that contain these cells, such as sperm, saliva, blood, vaginal secretions, perspiration, hair with roots, organs, bones, teeth, and skin. The DNA processed for fingerprinting is not of the genetic sort associated with observable characteristics such as eye color and height. Sections of this type of protein-coding DNA do not distinguish individuals from one another in a way that the non-coding

DNA does. The only exception to this is the observation of sex determined by the presence of the XX chromosomes in females and the XY chromosomes in males.

Areas of "junk DNA" however, exhibit a great deal of variability between individuals. Regions of it have been found to contain repeated sequences of base pairs. There are in fact, hundreds of thousands of these repeated sequences distributed on all chromosomes but the number of repeated sequences and the pattern of their distribution on each chromosome are unique in every individual except for identical twins. Sections of this non-coding DNA (referred to as *polymorphisms*) are extracted for examination and processed into an image, producing a fingerprint or profile.

The tandemly repeated sequences of DNA are typically classified into different groups based on the size of the repeat region. Regions with repeats of 9 to 80 base pairs are referred to as Variable Number Tandem Repeats (*VNTRs*, also known as *minisatellites*) while regions that contain 2 to 5 base pair repeats are called Short Tandem Repeats (*STRs*, also known as *microsatellites*).

STR analysis is currently a popular method of DNA typing in forensic science and is the technique described below. It examines smaller regions of repeated sequences and therefore does not require large quantities of DNA. It can also use DNA that has degraded. Combined with a technique called *Polymerase Chain Reaction* (PCR), STR analysis has made DNA typing more reliable, less time consuming, and with a higher degree of discrimination.

Establishing Standard Protocol for the Use of DNA

The introduction of DNA analysis into US courts in 1988 provoked much debate and controversy in both the legal and scientific arenas. Scientists argued over statistical calculations and practical applications, while biotech start-up companies with no experience in forensic science marred early DNA typing with poorly defined procedures. (Lander and Budowle, 1994). In 1989, a criminal case involving DNA analysis was actually thrown out because scientists for both the prosecution and the defense decided in a joint statement that the evidence was unacceptable due to poor processing (Lander, 1998). Nonetheless, DNA typing was recognized as a spectacular new technology that promised to redefine the field of genetics research and criminalistics.

Laboratory standards had not been established prior to the introduction of DNA typing as a forensic science. As such, the policy governing its use in a court of law was ambiguous. Expert testimony allowed for the testimony to state only the mathematical probability of an individual's positively matching a sample and whether the suspect could be excluded or not. Stating that an individual's DNA profile positively matched the evidence analysed was not permitted. The technology was still very new and scientists were using different methods with different standards and matching rules (rules regarding whether two samples matched).

Within a few years of its introduction into courts, the use of forensic DNA typing began increasing at a rapid pace. A variety of methods were developed, and private laboratories began providing DNA typing services to law enforcement officials offering expert witnesses to translate laboratory results, and con-

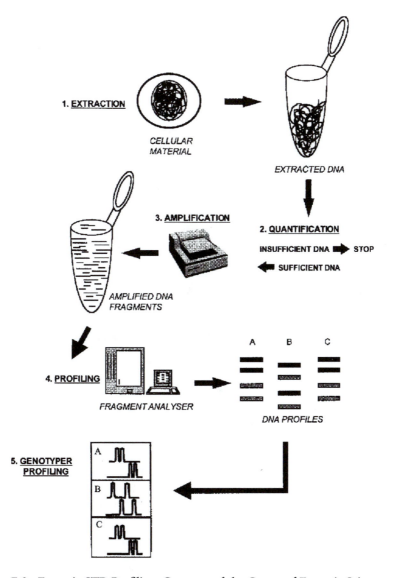

Diagram 7-2. Forensic STR Profiling. Courtesy of the Centre of Forensic Sciences.

1. DNA is extracted chemically from the sample by breaking down the components of the rest of the cell in order to isolate the DNA from the nucleus.

2-3. Copies of the DNA are made using the PCR technique (often referred to as PCR amplification). It is a fast technique which uses an enzyme for making an unlimited number of copies of DNA from different samples. This enables a lab to generate enough DNA from minute or degraded samples, such as saliva from an envelope or an old blood stain found on an article of clothing. PCR amplification is highly sensitive and must be done under sterile conditions, since the DNA being copied can easily be contaminated by foreign DNA, for example, in a technician's sneeze.

4-5. Steps 4 and 5 analyze the extracted DNA fragments of interest i.e. fragments taken from the same regions on a particular chromosome in different individuals. The most common method for analyzing these fragments is through what is called electrophoretic analysis.

sultants for attorneys. High profile criminal cases detailed the intricacies of DNA typing and went into great length describing the statistical probabilities of various matches. Yet a standard protocol regarding the use of such highly personal and sensitive information was still not in place, and many of the same questions regarding reliability, interpretation, and validity were still being raised by the scientific and legal communities.

Responding to these issues, the National Research Council Committee from the National Academy of Sciences put together a comprehensive report on DNA technology in forensic science in 1992. In it the committee addressed issues such as the applicability and appropriateness of the use of DNA technology for forensic use and the need to develop standards for collecting, analyzing, and presenting data. Furthermore, the report called for DNA typing procedures to have built-in measures that would ensure stringent procedures, confidentiality and consistency in the field (The NRC Report, 1992) because of the possibilities for its misuse and/or misinterpretation. Laboratories would be required to provide a detailed description of their typing method with a precise and objective matching rule and to undergo regular, mandatory proficiency tests. In other words, DNA typing methods would be tested internally to ensure that they were being done properly. Due to the power that DNA evidence carries in a court of law (the fact that it can now outweigh all other evidence in a trial), it became essential that high standards and a strict protocol governing its use be enacted.

By 1994 DNA typing was firmly established for use in forensic science and research began to accelerate; from a few research papers in the late1980s to more than 400 by the middle of 1994, combined with over 100 scientific conferences (Lander, 1998). Newer and quicker methods were continually being introduced, prompting three sets of laboratory guidelines to be released from the Technical Working Group on DNA Analysis Methods (TWGDAM). The FBI took a definitive stance towards developing procedures and initiated public discussion on the use of computer databases containing DNA profiles. It was no longer considered a controversial method of analysis but was touted as one of the greatest advances in forensic science since the development of fingerprinting in 1892.

In 1997, a new FBI policy went into effect allowing expert witnesses to testify definitively that a DNA sample matched that of a certain suspect, rather than stating it obliquely through statistical probability. The policy came about as a result of advances in testing which narrowed the odds a great deal, from a one in 1000 chance that another person besides the suspect had the same DNA profile to one in 260 billion!

Technological advances in the field of molecular genetics directly affected the controversy surrounding the use of forensic DNA typing, ultimately bringing an end to questions of its reliability. Highly sensitive testing methods can now process smaller and more degraded samples of DNA, enabling scientists to analyze a wider range of materials and thereby increase the amount of evidence admissible. Previously, items such as a stamp on an envelope, hair on a comb or a chewed up piece of gum, could never have been biologically linked to an individual. Currently they can, and within the world of forensic investigations, the genetic information provided by these items could quite possibly lead to a person's conviction for a crime or release from prison.

The DNA Database

In the late 1980s, the FBI had initiated talks aimed at establishing databanks of DNA profiles of convicted individuals, which could be stored and accessed when needed. The philosophy guiding the establishment of a databank was that a criminal could change his looks, change his address, and change his name but could never change his genetic profile. If evidence containing such information were present and if that information were available on a computer file, a "hit" (match) would be guaranteed.

In 1990, a software program called the *Combined DNA Index Systems* (CODIS) was developed and piloted by the FBI. CODIS is a double indexing system of DNA profiles, *The Convicted Offender Index*, which contains genetic profiles of sex offenders (and other violent crimes), and *The Forensic Index*, which contains profiles developed from crime scene evidence such as blood and semen. There is also information on the laboratory's identifier and the names of the individuals responsible for processing the DNA profile. Information such as an individual's criminal history, social security number, or details of criminal cases are not stored. The computer software program is designed to automatically search both of these indexes for matching DNA profiles (see CODIS Program Overview, 1998).

The FBI initially provided the software, installation, training and technical support free of charge to fourteen state and local DNA laboratories, enabling them to exchange and compare their data and possibly link serial crimes with known offenders. Within four years, CODIS had generated more than 400 matches which oftentimes led to the release of individuals for crimes they had not committed (see NIJ Research Report, 1996). The success with which the program was met allowed further research into databases to continue.

By October 1998, the FBI introduced the *National DNA Index System* (NDIS) the final level of the CODIS system which is currently installed in 94 laboratories in 41 states. The program now allows states to exchange and compare DNA profiles nationally as well as serving as a repository for DNA profiles submitted by states that are registered to participate (FBI National Press Office, 1998).

Although all 50 states have passed legislation requiring convicted offenders to provide blood samples for typing and entering into the database, eight states, as of June 1998, have not begun collecting samples, whereas other states have begun collecting but have not yet analyzed or entered the data. To date the FBI database holds DNA profiles of well over 250 000 convicted felons, while over 600,000 DNA samples have been collected nationally (CODIS Program Overview, 1998).

Controversy over the use of DNA during the last 10 years focused on how to apply it and how to interpret it. However, the controversy now surrounds the procedures for collecting DNA from convicted individuals. Some of the questions concern who should have to give blood samples and how those samples are to be handled, as well as who will have access to this information and whether it will be subject to abuse. Because DNA can provide more than just information on sequences of base pairs, such as medical characteristics, physical traits, and relatedness, some fear that this information carries the risks of discrimination. Throughout North America, civil libertarians are challenging the practice of having nationwide computers that store the genetic information of convicted persons and have raised issues relating to the right to genetic privacy.

The Federal DNA Identification Act of 1994 limits the database to DNA from convicted criminals. Access to database information is restricted to law enforcement officials, and a court order will be required to use this information in judicial proceedings. Furthermore, the location of the databank is kept secret for security purposes. When matches are made, laboratories responsible for the profiles are required to contact each other to verify the information exchanged. DNA analysts must then confirm the match once again before contacting the related law enforcement agency.

Despite a difficult beginning and the ongoing element of controversy, the success of the DNA database has been immediate. Within minutes of searching for possible matches, a convicted sex offender in Illinois was matched to a rape and an attempted murder in Wisconsin that had occurred nine years before. Success in the form of these direct "hits" is detailed in reports put out by the FBI and the National Institute of Justice (FBI CODIS Program Overview and the NIJ Report, 1996).

Every state is legally required to collect the DNA of sex offenders; however, various states have enacted laws allowing them also to collect (or not collect) from criminals charged with felons such as assault, murder, and offenses against children. What the state chooses to do with that information, i.e. analyze samples and enter them into the database, is another matter altogether.

Sophisticated technology has indeed allowed for faster and more accurate testing methods and the storing of information, culminating in a national system for identifying and apprehending criminals. However, the current type of technology and how it is driven can also be this system's downfall. Dr. Jeffreys himself has commented (*Science Watch,* 1995) that committing oneself to a large-scale database system entails being "trapped" in that technology. Once that technology changes, and it will, one cannot change the database without having to retype every individual in the system. Considering that there are hundreds of thousands of profiles that have taken years to collect and enter, and that the process is still ongoing, the idea of having to do it all over again is most daunting.

Section IV

New Applications

Chapter Eight

Human Rights and Forensic Anthropology

The application of forensic anthropology to the investigation of human rights violations has increased dramatically over the last 15 years. Countries throughout Latin America, Africa, the Middle East, and eastern Europe have been requesting the assistance of forensic anthropologists in recovering the remains of family members and spouses who were victims of civil war and past military regimes. The reinstatement of democratic governments in many of these countries, along with higher levels of public awareness and social action, have contributed to such an increase.

The first publicized use of forensic anthropology in a human rights mission was in 1984 when forensic anthropologist Dr. Clyde Snow traveled to Argentina as a consultant. He was asked to assist in identifying victims of the Argentinean War of 1974 to 1983 (Snow and Bihurriet, 1992). Many victims were identified, and subsequently a team of Argentine forensic anthropologists was formed, the *Equipo Argentino de Antropología Forense* (EAAF). Snow returned many times during the excavations and trained the team while testifying as an expert witness in an Argentine court of law.

Shortly thereafter a trend was established where forensic specialists from abroad could be called upon to recover and document physical evidence. The overall goal was to assist communities in bringing government and military members to trial for past crimes.

This chapter provides a brief account of the involvement of science in advancing the human rights cause. The history and mandate of various organizations are outlined along with a brief look at their contributions abroad. Following this is a discussion on the application of forensic anthropology to the investigation of human rights violations. For further reading on this topic see: Stover, 1985; Snow et al., 1992; Burns, 1991; Gibbons, 1992; Hannibal, 1992; Snow et al., 1989.

Science and Human Rights

In the United States a number of professional organizations have formed committees to investigate human rights issues. Lawyers, political scientists, physicians, psychiatrists, and civil engineers all advance human rights causes by writing letters to governments, organizing investigations, testifying in courts of law, and volunteering their services towards various programs and campaigns.

The Minnesota Lawyers International Human Rights Committee organized a group of forensic scientists in 1986 to write a document outlining the methods and procedures of investigating crimes against humanity. The document, known as the *Minnesota Protocol*, was adopted by the United Nations in 1991 (republished under the title: *Manual on the Effective Prevention and Investigation of Extra-Legal, Arbitrary and Summary Executions*). Currently it serves as an international manual for individuals investigating deaths resulting from human rights violations.

Another organization, the American Association for the Advancement of Science (AAAS), formed in 1976, created a branch organization called the Science and Human Rights Program (SHRP). The SHRP mandate is to encourage international respect for human rights outlined in the United Nations Universal Declaration of Human Rights. In response to requests from non-governmental organizations and citizen groups, the SHRP conducts casework and organizes humanitarian missions on behalf of scientists and health professionals around the world. Casework, reports, and missions are all based on the principle that basic human rights should be defended and encouraged as they are preconditions for any scientific endeavor.

Currently, the SHRP is the leader in scientific human rights missions. In turn, they have created many other resources accessible to AAAS affiliates and other human rights organizations. Since 1993 they have established the Human Rights Action Network which uses electronic mail to send out information regarding cases and issues of special interest. They now have a data center that publishes human rights reports and posts information on the International Center for Human Rights Research. Lastly, they have a human rights resource directory which provides links to human rights organizations worldwide.

Meanwhile, the Forensic Anthropology Team of Argentina (EAAF) has established its own precedent by becoming involved in other missions around the world. Since their formation in the mid 1980s, members have worked in countries such as South Africa, the Philippines, Iraq, and Bosnia. The team is now very much in demand due to their expertise in recovering and identifying bodies and presenting evidence for war tribunals.

Established professional organizations such as the ones described above are in a position to make unique contributions to human rights. Due to their interdisciplinary structure, many of these organizations are able to draw upon a multitude of resources. Lawyers, engineers, political scientists, doctors, geneticists, anthropologists, and many others contribute their expertise to the investigation of human rights violations worldwide. Oftentimes these violations have gone unreported and undocumented, and in many cases they still continue. The statements, reports, and publications that result from such investigations are designed to inform the public, to bring perpetrators to justice, and to alert governments that their transgressions have not gone unnoticed.

Forensic Anthropology and Human Rights Issues

The forensic anthropologist's involvement in human rights issues usually begins with some form of participation in a professional committee or with an invitation by an organization or government. They may even be called upon by the families of the deceased to assist in some form of recovery or identification. Forensic anthropologists primarily contribute by assisting with the excavation and death investigation work.

The differences, however, between forensic human rights casework and that of the standard legal investigation have to do with the perpetrators of the crimes and the scale of the work. In human rights casework, the perpetrators are often former government members or leaders, which often involve the police and/or military. The scale of the work is much greater, as there are sometimes mass graves to excavate and whole communities or villages to interview. As well, due to the nature of the crimes, the political climate of the region has a greater bearing on the success or failure of the mission than it would for the standard investigation.

Human rights missions for North American forensic anthropologists are primarily in foreign countries. Along with the process of disinterment, biological identification, and trauma analysis, they often work directly with individuals who have been searching for missing family members as well as with individuals from local neighborhoods and communities. This is done through the process of interviewing, recording eyewitness accounts, and may even involve taking blood samples (see Figs. 8-1 to 8-7). A special sensitivity to the laws and customs of that country is essential.

Forensic anthropologists join forces with other professionals in the field, as they do on other crime scenes. Forensic teams can include odontologists, botanists, archaeologists, radiologists, and geneticists working to reveal evidence of murder, summary executions, and torture. As in any crime scene, all evidence is documented, collected, and processed and then presented in a court of law through the testimony of expert witnesses. However, if this process is to flow without incident or interruption within the host country, that same sensitivity to culture applies. Knowing the local language, understanding factors such as the legal requirements and burial customs of that region as well as the area's history and demography increase the chance that the events surrounding a death can be interpreted accurately. It can also ensure that any evidence collected will not be confiscated.

The goal in many human rights cases is to prosecute the perpetrators. Under brutal dictatorships and military regimes, thousands of individuals have been arrested, abducted, and eventually executed. Their bodies were buried in mass graves, dumped into the sea, or simply went "missing." In Argentina alone, during the military regime lasting from 1976 to 1983, it was established that at least 10,000 people had "disappeared" (EAAF, 1998).

Legal prosecution of these perpetrators requires evidence. However, in human rights cases evidence is often based solely on verbal testimony from victims or witnesses. Corroborating this verbal testimony with physical evidence has been a major challenge (see Kirschner, 1994). Nevertheless, the application of the forensic sciences to human rights investigations has proven to be vital both in proving that these violations occurred and in obtaining some form of justice (Hannibal, 1992: 10).

Fig. 8-1. Collecting antemortem data from a relative of a disappeared person in El Salvador. Photo, M. Doretti. Reprinted with permission, EAAF, all rights reserved.

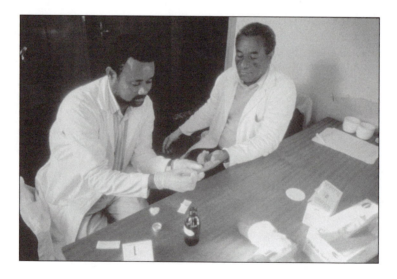

Fig. 8-2. Extracting a blood sample to compare DNA from relatives of disappeared people with that collected from skeletal remains in clandestine mass graves. Photo, M. Doretti. Reprinted with permission, EAAF, all rights reserved.

Fig. 8-3. Collecting information from relatives of Koreme victims. Physicians for Human Rights and Middle East Watch mission to Iraqi, Kurdistan, 1992. EAAF Archive, all rights reserved.

Fig. 8-4. EAAF member takes tri-dimensional measurement of each of the 141 individuals found in this mass grave. El Salvador. Photo, M. Doretti. Reprinted with permission, EAAF, all rights reserved.

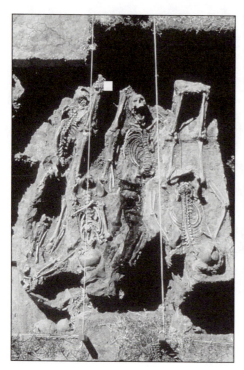

Fig. 8-5. (left) Excavation in Argentina. One of the mass graves containing remains of disappeared people. Argentina, 1988. Photo, M. Doretti. Reprinted with permission, EAAF, all rights reserved.

Fig. 8-6. (right) Archaeological techniques allowed recovery of evidence such as the rope used to tie this individual's wrists behind his back. Photo, EAAF Archive.\

Fig. 8-7. (below) Excavation recovered at least 143 individuals, 131 of which were under the age of 12. El Salvador, 1992. Photo, M. Doretti. Reprinted with permission, EAAF, all rights reserved.

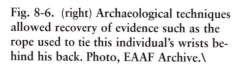

References

References

Allen, W.H., Merbs, C.F., and Birkby, W.H. 1985. Evidence for prehistoric scalping at Nuvakwewtaqa and Grasshopper Ruin, Arizona. In *Health and Disease in the Prehistoric Southwest*, C.F. Merbs and R.J. Miller (eds.). Arizona State University Anthropological Research Papers, No. 34, 23-42.

Anderson, J.E. 1969. *The Human Skeleton, A Manual for Archaeologists*. Ottawa: The National Museums of Canada.

Angel, J.L., Suchey, J.M., İşcan, M.Y., and Zimmerman, M.R. 1986. Age at death from the skeleton and viscera. In *Dating and Age Determination in Biological Materials*, M.R. Zimmerman and J.L. Angel (eds.), 179-120. London: Croom Helm.

Archer, K. 1998. 3-D Craniofacial Reconstruction (http://www.loonie.net/~karcher/thesis.html).

Ayers, H.G., Jantz, R.L., and Moore-Jansen, P.H. 1990. Giles and Elliot race discriminant functions revisited: A test using recent forensic cases. In *Skeletal Attribution of Race*, G.W. Gill and S. Rhine (eds.), 65-71. Albuquerque, NM: Maxwell Museum of Anthropology.

Ballantyne, J., Sensabaugh, G., and Witkowski, J. 1989. *DNA Technology and Forensic Science*. Cold Spring Harbor Laboratory Press.

Bass, W.M. 1995. *Human Osteology: A Laboratory and Field Manual of the Human Skeleton* (4th Ed.). Columbia, MO: Missouri Archaeological Society.

Bass, W.M. and Birkby, W.H. 1978. Exhumation: The method could make the difference. *FBI Law Enforcement Bulletin* 47(7):6-11.

Berryman, H., and Symes, S.A. 1998. Recognizing gunshot and blunt cranial trauma through fracture interpretation. In *Forensic Osteology: Advances in the Identification of Human Remains* (2nd Ed.), K.J. Reichs (ed.), 333-352. Springfield, IL: Charles C. Thomas.

Billings, P. 1992. *DNA on Trial: Genetic Identification and Criminal Justice*. Cold Spring Harbor Laboratory Press.

Binford, L.R. 1972. *An Archaeological Perspective*. New York. Seminar.

Blake, T. 1999. DNA Genotyping, or 'Whose finger was it anyway?' In *Hordeum* (http://hordeum.oscs.montana.edu/finger/finger.html). Bozeman, MT: Montana State University Dept. of Plant Sciences.

Brues, A. 1958. Identification of skeletal remains. *J. Criminal Law, Criminal Police Science*, 48:551-563.

Brothwell, D.R. 1981. *Digging Up Bones* (3rd Ed.). London: British Museum of Natural History.

Burchett, P.J. and Christensen, L.C. 1988. Estimating age and sex by using color, form, and alignment of anterior teeth. *Journal of Prosthetic Dentistry* 59:175-179.

Burns, K.R. 1991. Model protocol for disinterment and analysis of skeletal remains. In *Manual on the Effective Prevention and Investigation of Extra-Legal, Arbitrary and Summary Executions*. United Nations Publication, E.91.IV.1, 34-40.

Campbell, B.G. 1992. *Humankind Emerging* (5th Ed.). Boston: Little, Brown and Company.

Camps, F., Robinson, A., and Lucas, B.G. 1976. *Gradwohl's Legal Medicine*. Chicago: J. Wright.

Cartmill, M. 1999. The status of the race concept in physical anthropology. *American Anthropologist* 100(3):651-660.

Catts, E.P. 1990. Analyzing entomological data. In *Entomology and Death: A Procedural Guide*, E.P. Catts and N.H. Haskell (eds.), 124-137. Clemson, SC: Joyce's Print Shop.

Cherry, D.G. and Angel, J.L. 1977. Personality reconstruction from unidentified remains. *FBI Law Enforcement Bulletin* 48:12-15.

Committee on DNA Technology in Forensic Science. 1992. *DNA Technology in Forensic Science*. Washington, DC: National Research Council.

Courville, C.B. 1965a. War wounds of the cranium in the Middle Ages 1: As disclosed in the skeletal material from the Battle of Visby (1361). *Bull. Los Angeles Neurol. Soc.* 30:27-33.

Di Maio, V.J.M. 1993. *Gunshot Wounds: Practical Aspects of Firearms, Ballistics and Forensic Techniques*. Boca Raton, FL: CRC Press.

Dwight, T. 1878. *The Identification of the Human Skeleton. A Medico-legal Study*. Boston: Massachusetts Medical Society.

Dumont, E.R. 1986. Mid-facial tissue depths of white children: An aid to facial feature reconstruction. *Journal of Forensic Sciences* 34:1214-1221.

Eckert, W.G. (ed.). 1987. *The Forensic Sciences: An Introduction*. Wichita, KS: The Milton Helpern International Center for the Forensic Sciences.

Eckert, W.G. (ed.). 1997. *Introduction to Forensic Sciences* (2nd Ed.). Boca Raton, FL: CRC Press.

El-Najjar, M. and McWilliams, K.R. 1978. *Forensic Anthropology: The Structure, Morphology, and Variation of Human Bone and Dentition*. Springfield, IL: Charles C. Thomas.

Erickson, M.F. 1982. How "representative" is the Terry Collection? Evidence from the proximal femur. *American Journal of Physical Anthropology* 59:45-350.

Equipo Argentino de Antropología Forense. 1998. *The 1996-1997 Biannual Report*. New York: EAAF.

Evison, M.P., Finegan, O.M., and Blythe, T. 1998. Computerized 3-D facial reconstruction. In *Assemblage* (http://forensic.shef.ac.uk/assem/evison6.wrl).

Ferembach, D., Schwidetzky, I., and Stloukal, M. 1980. Recommendations for age and sex diagnoses of skeletons. *Journal of Human Evolution* 9:517-549.

Foster, K.R. and Huber, P.W. 1997. *Judging Science: Scientific Knowledge and the Federal Courts*. Cambridge, MA: MIT Press.

Freeman, M.D.A. and Reece, H. (eds.). 1998. *Science in Court*. Aldershot, England.

Frost, H.M. 1985. The "new bone": Some anthropological potentials. *Yearbook of Physical Anthropology* 28:211-226.

Galloway, A. 1997. The process of decomposition: A model from the Arizona-Sonoran Desert. In *Forensic Taphonom: The Postmortem Fate of Human Remains*, W.D. Haglund and M.H. Sorg (eds.), 139-150. Boca Raton, FL: CRC Press.

Galloway, A., Birkby, W.H., Jones, A.M., Henry, T.E., and Parks, B.O. 1989. Decay rates of human remains in an arid environment. *Journal of Forensic Sciences* 34:607-616.

Galloway, A. 1988. Estimating actual height in the older individual. *Journal of Forensic Sciences* 33:126-136.

George, R.M. 1987. The lateral craniographic method of facial reconstruction. *Journal of Forensic Sciences* 32:1305-1330.

Gerasimov, M.M. 1968. *The Face Finder*. London: Hutchinson and Co.

Gerber, S.M. 1983. *Chemistry and Crime: From Sherlock Holmes to Today's Courtroom*. American Chemical Society.

Gibbons, A. 1992. Scientists search for the "disappeared" in Guatemala. *Science* 257:479.

Giles, E. and Elliot, O. 1962. Race identification from cranial measurements. *Journal of Forensic Sciences* 7:147-57.

Giles, E. and Elliot, O. 1963. Sex determination by discriminant function analysis of crania. *American Journal of Physical Anthropology* 21:53-68.

Giles, E. and Hutchinson, D.L. 1991. Stature and age-related bias in self-reported stature. *Journal of Forensic Science* 36(3):765-780.

Gill, G.W. 1998. Craniofacial criteria in the skeletal attribution of race. In *Forensic Osteology: Advances in the Identification of Human Remains* (2nd Ed.), K.J. Reichs (ed.), 293-317. Springfield, IL: Charles C. Thomas.

Gill, G.W., and Rhine, S. (eds.). 1990. *Skeletal Attribution of Race*. Anthropology Papers No. 4. Maxwell Museum of Anthropology.

Gilbert, B.M. 1973. Misapplication to females of the standard for aging the female os pubis. *American Journal of Physical Anthropology* 38:39-40.

Gilbert, B.M. and McKern, T.W. 1973. A method for aging the female os pubis. *American Journal of Physical Anthropology* 38:31-38.

Goodman, A.H., and Armelagos, G.J. 1996. The resurrection of race: The concept of race in physical anthropology in the 1990s. In *Race and Other Misadventures: Essays in Honor of Ashley Montagu in His Ninetieth Year*, L.T. Reynolds and L. Lieberman (eds.), 174-186. Dix Hills, NY:General Hall.

Gurdjian, E.S., Webster, J.E., and Lissner, H.R. 1950. The mechanism of skull fracture. *Radiology* 54:313-339.

Haglund, W.D. 1998. The scene and the context: contributions of the forensic anthropologist. *Forensic Osteology: Advances in the Identification of Human Remains* (2nd ed.), K.J. Reichs (ed.). Springfield, IL: Charles C. Thomas.

Haglund, W.D. 1998. Guidelines to scene processing of decomposed and skeletal remains. *Forensic Osteology: Advances in the Identification of Human Remains* (2nd Ed.), K.J. Reichs (ed.), 57-62. Springfield, IL: Charles C. Thomas.

Haglund, W.D. and Sorg, M.H. (eds.). 1997. *Forensic Taphonomy: The Postmortem Fate of Human Remains*. Boca Raton, FL: CRC Press.

Halpern, M. 1954. *Legal Medicine and Toxicology* (2nd Ed.). Appleton-Century Croft.

Hannibal, K. 1992. *Taking Up the Challenge: The Promotion of Human Rights, A Guide for the Scientific Community*. Science and Human Rights Program, American Association for the Advancement of Science, Publication 92-32S.

Harkness, W.H., Ramsey, W.C., and Ahmadi, B. 1984. Principles of fractures and dislocations. In *Fractures in Adults, Volume I*, C.A. Rockwood and D.P. Dean (eds.), 1-18. Philadelphia: J.B. Lippincott Co.

His, W. 1895. Anatomische Forschungen ueber Johann Sebastian Bach Gebeine und Antlitz' nebst Bemerkungen ueber dessen Bilder. *Abhandlungen der Saechsischen Gesellschaft und Wissenschaften zu Leipz* 22:379-420.

Hodson, G., Lieberman, L.S., and Wright, P. 1985. In Vivo measurements of facial thicknesses in American Caucasoid children. *Journal of Forensic Sciences* 30:1100-1112.

Hooton, E.A. 1943. Medicolegal aspects of physical anthropology. *Clinics* 1:1612-1624.

Hunt, E.E. and Gleiser, I. 1955. The estimation of age and sex of preadolescent children from bone and teeth. *American Journal of Physical Anthropology* 13(3):479-487.

İşcan, M.Y. 1981a. Concepts in teaching forensic anthropology. *Medical Anthropology Newsletter* 13(1):10-12.

İşcan, M.Y. and Helmer, R.P. (eds.). 1993. *Forensic Analysis of the Skull*. New York: Wiley-Liss.

İşcan, M.Y. and Loth, S.R. 1989. Osteological manifestations of age in the adult. In *Reconstruction of Life from the Skeleton*, M.Y. Iscan and K.A.R. Kennedy (eds.), 23-40. New York: Alan R. Liss.

İşcan, M.Y. and Kennedy, K.A.R. (eds.). 1989. *Reconstruction of Life From the Skeleton*. New York: Alan R. Liss.

İşcan, M.Y., Loth, S.R., and Wright, R.K. 1984a. Metamorphosis at the sternal rib end: A new method to estimate age at death in white males. *American Journal of Physical Anthropology* 65(2):147-156.

İşcan, M.Y., Loth, S.R., and Wright, R.K. 1985. Age estimation from the rib by phase analysis: White females. *Journal of Forensic Science* 30(3):853-863.

İşcan, M.Y., Loth, S.R., and Wright, R.K. 1987. Racial variation in the sternal extremity of the rib and its effect on age determination. *Journal of Forensic Science* 32(2):452-466.

Jeffreys, A.J., Wilson, V., and Thein, S.L. 1985a. Hypervariable minisatellite regions in human DNA. *Nature* 314(6006):67-73.

Jeffreys, A.J., Wilson, V., and Thein, S.L. 1985b. Individual-specific fingerprints of human DNA. *Nature* 316(6023):76-9.

Kaye, B.H. 1995. *Science and the Detective: Selected readings in forensic science.* Weinheim, NY: VCH.

Katz, D. and Suchey, J.M. 1986. Age determination of the male os pubis. *American Journal of Physical Anthropology* 69:427-435.

Kennedy, K.A.R. 1989. Skeletal markers of occupational stress. In *Reconstruction of Life from the Skeleton*, M.Y. İşcan and K.A.R. Kennedy (eds.), 129-160. New York: Alan R. Liss.

Kollman, J. 1898. Die Weichteile des Gesichts und Persistenz der Rassen. *Anatomischer Anzeiger* 15:165-177.

Kirk, P.L. 1960. *Crime Investigation: Physical Evidence and the Police Laboratory.* New York: Interscience Publishers.

Kirschner, R.H. 1994. The application of the forensic sciences to human rights investigations. *The International Journal of Medicine and Law* 13:451-460.

Krawczak, M. and Schmidtke, J. 1998. *DNA Fingerprinting.* BIOS Scientific Publishers Limited.

Krogman, W.M. 1939. A guide to the identification of human skeletal material. *FBI Law Enforcement Bulletin* 8(8):3-31.

Krogman, W.M. 1943. Role of the physical anthropologist in the identification of human skeletal remains. *FBI Law Enforcement Bulletin* 12(4):17-40; 12(5):12-28.

Krogman, W.M. 1946. The reconstruction of the living head from the skull. *FBI Law Enforcement Bulletin* 15:1-8.

Krogman, W.M. 1962. *The Human Skeleton in Forensic Medicine.* Springfield, IL: Charles C. Thomas

Krogman, W.M. and İşcan, M.Y. 1986. Restoration of physiognomy. In *The Human Skeleton in Forensic Medicine.* Springfield, IL: Charles C. Thomas.

Kvaal, S.I. and Solheim, T. 1995. Incremental lines in human dental cementum in relation to age. *European Journal of Oral Science* 103:225-230.

Lander, E.S. 1998. Standards for DNA identification practice. In *DNA on the Witness Stand.* Genentech, Inc. (http://www.accessexcellence.org/AB/WYW/lander/lander_5.html).

Lander, E.S. and Budowle, B. 1994. DNA fingerprinting dispute laid to rest. *Nature* 371 (October).

Lebedinskaya, G.V., Balueva, T.S., and Veselovskaya, E.V. 1993. *Principles of facial reconstruction in Forensic Analysis of the Skull*, M.Y. İşcan and R.P. Helmer (eds.), New York: Wiley-Liss.

Lindemaier, G., Schuller, E., Müller, K., and Grabmann, S. 1989. Lebensalter und Zahnzahlein Hilfsmittel zur Identifizierung unbekannter Leichen. *Beitr Gerichtl Med* 47:515-518.

Lovejoy, C.O. and Heiple, K.G. 1981. The analysis of fractures in skeletal populations with an example from the Libben site, Ottawa County, Ohio. *American Journal of Physical Anthropology* 55:529-541.

Lovejoy, C.O., Meindl, R.S., Pryzbeck, T.R., and Mensforth, R.P. 1985. Chronological metamorphosis of the auricular surface of the ilium: A new method for the determination of adult skeletal age at death. *American Journal of Physical Anthropology* 68:15-28.

Mann, R.W., Bass, W.M., and Meadows, L. 1990. Time since death and decomposition of the human body: Variables and observations in case and experimental field studies. *Journal of Forensic Sciences* 35:103-111.

Maples, W.R. and Browning, M. 1995. *Dead Men Do Tell Tales: The Strange and Fascinating Cases of a Forensic Anthropologist.* New York: Doubleday.

Meadows, L. and Jantz, R.L. 1995. Allometric secular change in the long bones from the 1800s to the present. *Journal of Forensic Sciences* 40:762-767.

McElwee, J. 1998. Re: Redundant DNA. Posted in *The Mad Scientist Network*. Molecular and Cellular Biology, University of Washington-Seattle (Madsci. org/posts/archives/dec98).

Meindl R.S. and Lovejoy, C.O. 1985. Ectocranial suture closure: A revised method for the determination of skeletal age at death and blind tests of its accuracy. *American Journal of Physical Anthropology* 68:57-66.

Meindl, R.S., Lovejoy, C.O., Mensforth, R.P., and Walker, R.A., 1985. A revised method of age determination using the os pubis, with a review and tests of accuracy of other current methods of pubis symphyseal aging. *American Journal of Physical Anthropology* 68:29-45.

Merbs, C.F. 1989. Trauma. In *Reconstruction of Life from the Skeleton*, M.Y. İşcan and K.A.R. Kennedy (eds.), 161-189. New York: Alan R. Liss.

McKern, T.W. and Stewart, T.W. 1957. *Skeletal age changes in young American males: Analysed from the standpoint of age identification.* Environmental Protection Research Division, Technical Report No. EP-45. Natick, MA: Quartermaster Research and Development Center, U.S. Army.

Micozzi, M.S. 1991. *Taphonomy of Human and Animal Remains: Systematic Study of Postmortem Changes.* Springfield, IL: Charles C. Thomas, Publisher.

Miller, H. 1995. *Traces of Guilt: Forensic Science and the Fight Against Crime.* London: BBC Books.

National Institute of Justice Report. 1996. *Convicted by Juries, Exonerated by Science: Case Studies in the Use of DNA Evidence to Establish Innocence After Trial.*

National Institute of Standards and Technology (U.S.) Office of Law Enforcement Standards. 1998. *Forensic Laboratories: Handbook for facility planning, design, construction, and moving.* United States Office of Justice Programs.

Nawrocki, S.P. 1998. Regression formulae for estimating age at death from cranial suture closure. In *Forensic Osteology: Advances in the Identification of Human Remains* (2nd Ed.), K.J. Reichs (ed.), 276-292. Springfield, IL: Charles C. Thomas.

Nemeskéri, J., Harsányi, L., and Acsádi, G. 1960. Methoden zur diagnose des lebensalters von skelettfunden. *Anthropol Anz* 24:70-95.

Nickell, J. and Fischer, J.F. 1999. *Crime Science: Methods of Forensic Detection*. Lexington: University Press of Kentucky.

Ousley, S.D. 1995. Should we estimate "biological" or forensic stature? *Journal of Forensic Sciences* 40:768-773.

Ousley, S.D. and Jantz, R.L. 1998. The forensic data bank: documenting skeletal trends in the United States. In *Forensic Osteology: Advances in the Identification of Human Remains* (2nd Ed.), K.J. Reichs (ed.), 441-458. Springfield, IL: Charles C. Thomas.

Pragg, J. and Neave, R. 1997. *Making Faces: Using Forensic and Archaeological Evidence*. London: British Museum Press.

Proctor, A., Dale, M., and Williams, J. 1998. *Evidence: The True Witness* (http://library.advanced.org/17049/...cgi-bin/document_get.cgi?path=/DNA).

Reichs, K.J. 1998. Postmortem dismemberment: recovery, analysis and interpretation. In *Forensic Osteology: Advances in the Identification of Human Remains* (2nd Ed.), K.J. Reichs (ed.), 353-370. Springfield, IL: Charles C. Thomas.

Reichs, K.J. 1999. *Death Du Jour*. New York: Scribner.

Rhine, S. 1998. *Bone Voyage: A Journey in Forensic Anthropology*. Albuquerque: University of New Mexico Press.

Rodriguez, W.C. and Bass, W.M. 1983. Insect activity and it's relationship to decay rates of human cadavers in East Tennessee. *Journal of Forensic Sciences* 28:423-432.

Rösing, F.W. and Kvaal, S.I. 1998. Dental age in adults—a review of estimation methods. In *Dental Anthropology: Fundamentals, Limits, and Prospects*, K.W. Alt, F.W. Rösing, and M. Teschler-Nicola (eds.), 443-468. Wien and New York: Springer.

Saferstein, R. 1981. *Criminalistics: An Introduction to Forensic Science*. Englewood Cliffs, NJ: Prentice-Hall.

Saferstein, R. (ed.) 1982. Forensic Science Handbook. Englewood Cliffs, NJ: Prentice-Hall.

Saunders, G. 1987. Fiftieth anniversary of the crime detection laboratories. *The RCMP Gazette* 49(11).

Schoenly, K. 1992. A statistical analysis of successional patterns in carrion-arthropod assemblages: Implications for forensic entomology and determination of the postmortem interval. *Journal of Forensic Sciences* 37:1489-1513.

Schour, I. and Massler, M. 1941. The development of the human dentition. *Journal of the American Dental Association* 28:1153-1160

Science Watch. *Sir Alec Jeffreys on DNA profiling and minisatellites.* Institute for Scientific Information Newsletter 6[4] (April1995):3-4.

Shahrom, A.W., Vanezis, P., Chapman, R.C., Gonzales, A., Blenkinsop, C., and Rossi, M.I. 1996. Techniques in facial identification: Computer-aided facial reconstruction using a laser scanner and video superimposition. *International Journal of Legal Medicine* 108(4):194-200.

Singer, R. 1953. Estimation of age from cranial suture closure: A report on its unreliability. *Journal of Forensic Medicine* 1:52-59.

Sledzik, P.S. 1997. Forensic taphonomy: Postmortem decomposition and decay. In *Forensic Taphonomy: The Postmortem Fate of Human Remains*, W.D. Haglund and M.H. Sorg (eds.), 109-119. Boca Raton, FL: CRC Press.

Sledzik, P.S. and Micozzi, M.S. 1997. Autopsied, embalmed, and preserved human remains: Distinguishing features in forensic and historic contexts. In *Forensic Taphonomy: The Postmortem Fate of Human Remains*, W.D. Haglund and M.H. Sorg (eds.), 109-119. Boca Raton, FL: CRC Press.

Smith, K.G.V. 1986. *A Manual of Forensic Entomology.* Ithaca: Cornell University Press.

Snow, C.C., Gatliff, B., and McWilliams, K.R. 1970. Reconstruction of facial features from the skull; an evaluation of its usefulness in forensic anthropology. *American Journal of Physical Anthropology* 33:221-228.

Snow, C.C., Stover, E., and Hannibal, K. 1989. Scientists as detectives investigating human rights. *Technology Review* 92:43-51.

Snow, C.C. and Bihurriet, M.J. 1992. An epidemiology of homicide: ningún nombre burials in the province of Buenos Aires from 1970 to 1984. In *Human Rights and Statistics: Getting the Record Straight*, T.B. Jabine, and R.P. Claude, 328-364. Philadelphia: University of Pennsylvania Press.

Spitz, W.U. (ed.) 1993. *Medicolegal Investigation of Death* (3rd Ed.). Springfield, IL: Charles C. Thomas.

Steele, D.G. 1970. Estimation of stature from fragments of long limb bones. In *Personal Identification in Mass Disasters*, T.D. Stewart (ed.), 85-97. Washington, DC: National Museum of Natural History.

Steele, D.G. and Bramblett, C.A. 1988. *The Anatomy and Biology of the Human Skeleton.* College Station, TX: Texas A&M University Press.

Stewart, T.D. 1948. Medico-legal aspects of the skeleton 1: Sex, age, race, and stature. *American Journal of Physical Anthropology* 6:315-322.

Stewart, T.D. 1951. What the bones tell. *FBI Law Enforcement Bulletin* 20(2):2-5, 19.

Stewart, T.D. 1979. *Essentials of Forensic Anthropology.* Springfield, IL: Charles C. Thomas.

Stott, G.G., Sis, R.F., and Levy, B.M. 1981. Cemental annulation as an age criterion in forensic dentistry. *Journal of Dental Research* 61:814-817.

Stover, E. 1985. Scientists search for Argentina's missing. *Clearinghouse Report on Science and Human Rights* VII(2):1-3.

Stuart-Macadam, P.L. 1989. Nutritional deficiency diseases: A survey of scurvy, rickets, and iron-deficiency anemia. In *Reconstruction of Life From the Skeleton*, M.Y. İşcan and K.A.R. Kennedy (eds.), 201-222. New York: Alan R. Liss.

Suchey, J.M. and Katz, D. 1986. *Skeletal age standards derived from an extensive multiracial sample of modern Americans.* Paper presented at the Fifty-Fifth Annual Meeting of the American Association of Physical Anthropologists, Albuquerque.

Suchey, J.M., Owings, P.A., Wiseley, D.V., and Noguchi, T.T. 1984. Skeletal aging of unidentified persons. In *Human Identification: Case Studies in Forensic Anthropology*, T.A. Rathbun and J.E. Buikstra (eds.). Springfield, IL: Charles C Thomas.

Suchey, J.M., Wiseley, D.V., and Katz, D. 1986. Evaluation of the Todd and McKern-Stewart methods for aging the male os pubis. In *Forensic Osteology: Advances in the Identification of Human Remains*, K.J. Reichs (ed.). Springfield, IL: Charles C Thomas.

Templeton, A.R. 1999. Human races: A genetic and evolutionary perspective. *American Anthropologist* 100(3):632-650.

Thomas, William A. 1974. *Scientists in the Legal System; Tolerated Meddlers or Essential Contributors?* Ann Arbor Science Publishers Inc.

Thorwald, J. 1965. *The Century of the Detective*. New York: Harcourt, Brace and World.

Thorwald, J. 1967. *Crime and Science: The New Frontier in Criminology*. New York: Harcourt, Brace and World.

Todd, T.W. 1920. Age changes in the pubic bone: I. The male white pubis. *American Journal of Physical Anthropology* 3:285-334.

Todd, T.W. 1921a. Age changes in the pubic bone: II. The pubis of the male Negro-white hybrid; III. The pubis of the white female; IV. The pubis of the female Negro-white hybrid. *American Journal of Physical Anthropology* 4:1-70.

Trotter, M. and Gleser, G.C. 1952. Estimation of stature from long bones of American whites and negroes. *American Journal of Physical Anthropology* 10:463-514.

Trotter, M. 1970. Estimation of stature from intact long limb bones. In *Personal Identification in Mass Disasters*, T.D. Stewart (ed.), 71-83. Washington, DC: National Museum of Natural History.

Ubelaker, D.H. 1996. *Skeletons Testify: Anthropology in Forensic Science*. AAPA Luncheon Address. Yearbook of Physical Anthropology 39:229-244.

Ubelaker, D.H. and O'Donnell, G. 1992. Computer assisted facial reconstruction. *Journal of Forensic Sciences* 37:155-62.

Ubelaker, D.H. 1978. *Human Skeletal Remains: Excavation, Analysis, Interpretation*. Washington, DC: Taraxacum.

U.S. Department of Justice, Federal Bureau of Investigation. 1998. *CODIS Program Overview*. Washington, DC, October 8.

U.S. Department of Justice, Federal Bureau of Investigation. 1998. *DNA Database Press Release*. National Press Office. Washington, DC, October 13.

Vanezis, P., Blowes, R.W., Linney, A.D., Tan, A.C., Richards, R., and Neave, R. 1989. Application of 3-D computer graphics for facial reconstruction and comparison with sculpting techniques. *Forensic Science International* 42:69-84.

Wallman, K.K. and Hodgdon, J. 1977. Race and ethnic standards for federal statistics and administrative reporting. *Statistical Reporter* 77(10):450-454.

Weihs, F. 1964. *Science Against Crime*. New York: Collier Books.

Welcker, H. 1883. *Schiller's Schädel und todenmaske, nebst mittheilungen über Schädel und todenmaske Kants*. Braunschweig.

Welcker, H. 1884. Der Schadel Rafaels und die Rafaelportraits. *Arch Anthropol* 15:417-440

Wilson, E.S. and Katz, F.N. 1969. Stress fracture: An analysis of 250 consecutive cases. *Radiology* 92:481-486.

Index

DATE DUE

Mar 30/04					